THE FORGOTTEN LANDSCAPES OF THE
YORKSHIRE WOLDS

THE FORGOTTEN LANDSCAPES OF THE
YORKSHIRE WOLDS

CHRIS FENTON-THOMAS

TEMPUS

Photographs by Peter Fenton unless otherwise credited

First published 2005

Tempus Publishing Limited
The Mill, Brimscombe Port,
Stroud, Gloucestershire, GL5 2QG
www.tempus-publishing.com

British Library Cataloguing in Publication Data.
A catalogue record for this book is available from the British Library.

ISBN 0 7524 3346 6

Typesetting and origination by Tempus Publishing Limited
Printed in Great Britain

CONTENTS

ACKNOWLEDGEMENTS

The research work for this book was part of a PhD thesis, supervised by Andrew Fleming and Mark Edmonds at the University of Sheffield. They have both had a big influence on the way I have approached and written about this landscape. Whilst at Sheffield, I was lucky to have been surrounded by other people also working on the Wolds and the work of Bill Bevan, Mel Giles, Pat Wagner, Mike Parker-Pearson and Colin Hayfield has contributed a great deal to this story. I owe many of the ideas in the book to the writings of Harold Fox, Richard Bradley, Tim Ingold, Tom Williamson and Chris Wickham.

I am grateful to all copyright holders who agreed to let me use their photographs or illustrations and especially to Derek Brooks for taking the overhead shots of the excavations at Melton. Liz Chamberlin at the Humber Archaeology Partnership was very helpful. Thanks also to the many people who took time to fill in the questionnaires and send them back with such candid comments.

Finally, special thanks to Peter for taking the wonderful photos and also to Claire for tireless proof reading.

ONE

ARCHAEOLOGY, LANDSCAPE AND LONG-TERM HISTORY

That part of it towards the sea and the river Derwent is pretty fruitful, but the middle is nothing but a heap of mountains, called Yorkeswold, which signifies Yorkshire Hills. (Camden, 1586 *Britannia*)

HISTORIC COUNTRYSIDE

The countryside means many different things to the people who live in England today. For a lot of us it is a place of retreat from the working week, spent in traffic jams or office blocks. For others it is home, where animals are raised and crops grown and it is hard work to make the land provide a living wage. Some folks see the English countryside as traditional and reliable whilst others make use of the rural freedom to live a different life, away from pollution and consumerism. This landscape means many things and takes a bewildering variety of forms. For instance, many parts of the south-west have an organic feel with deep sunken lanes winding through pasture fields lined by thick hedges and stands of woodland. This cannot be more different than the open plains of Cambridgeshire or Lincolnshire where large rectangular arable fields are bordered by short hawthorn hedges and wide straight and level roads. Whatever the landscape means, the look of the place today has been moulded and shaped over many centuries. These differences across the country are not caused by soil changes or climate, but by history.

The differences in the appearance of landscapes are mirrored by the different histories they have enjoyed. Some areas, like the East Midlands and parts of Yorkshire, were altered dramatically during the eighteenth- and nineteenth-century enclosures. They contain few visible ancient features on the surface. Other landscapes have stayed much the same for many centuries and here the history stands proud above the ground. In some parts of Cornwall, for instance, there has been very little change in the layout of fields or lanes. The location of hamlets and farms in the modern landscape is often the same as settlement sites from many centuries past. In some places, the layout of fields today may be the same as that in late prehistory. In the extreme south-west of England and across Wales and Scotland, many names of rivers, hills, fields or settlements also remain unchanged. In East Anglia there is a similar situation. Here it is possible to study maps from the eighteenth century and to trace the lines of very ancient field systems from them. In some cases, the lines of their boundaries have not been altered since before the Roman Conquest. However, the farming system, of which they form part, has altered beyond all recognition.

In some parts of England, it is possible to obtain a tenth-century document describing the boundaries of an Anglo-Saxon estate territory. These perambulations take the reader on a journey from landmark to landmark round the boundaries of the estate. In many cases these boundaries still remain in the modern landscape and can be followed on foot. In other parts of the country, we can walk the hills and literally bump into the upstanding remains of ancient walls and buildings. Upland areas like Dartmoor, the Pennines or the North York Moors have not been occupied or farmed since the second or first millennium BC and here the derelict remains of fields, lanes and settlement sites still survive.

This sort of survival is characteristic of ancient or woodland countryside and these areas are considered to be 'landscapes of continuity'. The survival of many ancient sites and features gives the landscape historian a challenge to disentangle the old from the new and to create a history based on the visible traces. In 'planned countryside', things are very different. They have seen many periods of alteration which have obscured the past traces of hedges, fields and lanes and laid new ones out afresh. This means that very few ancient features such as tracks or field boundaries are still being used. They have been erased and now lie concealed beneath the modern patterns of fields and settlements. This lack of evidence on the surface presents us with a challenge as it forces us to use archaeological techniques to identify and trace ancient landscape features.

1 A view down Holm Dale, south of Fridaythorpe

THE LANDSCAPE OF THE WOLDS

The Yorkshire Wolds has all the appearance of a planned countryside. Here is a landscape of large rectangular fields bounded by short hawthorn hedges. The roads are straight and broad with wide verges and they lead directly from village to village. This land is overwhelmingly arable and, since the Second World War, the area has become intensively farmed on an ever-increasing scale (*2*). The Wolds landscape was created during the eighteenth and nineteenth centuries by enclosure. This book is about the history of this landscape and how it once possessed a very different character. Today's managed arable fields were once wild grassland waste, the preserve of shepherds and wanderers. The story of the Wolds unfolds over a long time and we will join it at about 1000 BC. From here, we will trace the development of the landscape throughout the first millennium BC, Roman period and Middle Ages to the present day.

If we had travelled across the Wolds in 1700, we would have seen a very different countryside to that encountered 200 years later in 1900. Topographers and agriculturalists took an interest in the place during this time and have described the agricultural improvements that were made. In 1700, the villages were surrounded by large open fields that had not changed much since the Middle Ages. Enclosure was designed to improve the efficiency of farming and turn a profit from the land. It

2 Traces of the modern arable landscape on the slopes of Cow Dale, between Huggate and Wetwang

signalled the end of the collective farming system where each household had a stake in the land and its harvest. At enclosure the land was allocated to individual owners who could use the new agricultural techniques to make a profit for themselves.

Parliamentary enclosure took place in areas where the open fields remained. In other parts of the country, the land had been gradually enclosed throughout the later Middle Ages and there was no need for the radical transformations made by the enclosure commissioners (5). On the Wolds, roads were re-aligned, fields laid out and new farms and plantations constructed between villages. This period created the look of the Wolds countryside today. One agriculturalist writing in 1769 recorded that:

> Between Market Weighton and Beverley, I observed several warrens, which must raise the wonder of every traveller, to see such good land left to so woeful an use; the turf is exceedingly rich and fine, and the plentiful crops of thistles scattered about it, prove the natural goodness of the soil … About Bishop Burton is some of the most extraordinary open field land I have met with; for it let while open at 18s and 20s an acre; and now a bill of enclosure has passed, it is said to raised to near 30s per acre.

The changes took place over a century and occurred within each township area at different times. For this reason, the changes in some townships were more radical than others. In some cases, the entire landscape was re-planned and apportioned, whilst in others, the changes were not radical enough to obliterate every ancient feature so some tracks and boundaries were re-used.

The townships found on the chalk Wolds were enclosed more radically than the areas to the east and west where this process had been ongoing for centuries. In 1720, Isaac Leatham wrote:

> I observed the middle of this riding or division of Yorkshire is very thin of towns and, consequently, of people being overspread with Woulds, that is to say plains and downs, like those of Salisbury; on which they feed great numbers of sheep, and breed also a great many black cattle and horses; ... But the east and west is populous and rich and full of towns, the one lying on the sea coast and the other upon the river Derwent.

The changes of enclosure meant many upstanding archaeological sites were lost at this time as open commons were enclosed and ploughed. This made it more difficult for archaeologists and landscape historians to see the past. As expressed by Reverend E.M. Cole in 1890:

> The beginning of the present century [nineteenth] found the larger portion of the high wolds of East Yorkshire still unenclosed. Large tracts of open common, dotted here and there with furze, afforded herbage for cattle and shelter for the great Bustard, Curlew and Thick-Knee. Then came the Inclosure Act; then the divine turnip; and soon the wild wastes were turned into profitable sheep farms and for many years the 'wool paid the rent'. All this however could not be done without sad destruction to the numberless entrenchments, which covered this part of Yorkshire. A few indeed have been preserved where a plantation or a hedge has offered protection, but the greater number have succumbed to the plough and can only be traced now by artful methods, which for the present we keep concealed from the gaze of the curious.

Barrows and field boundaries were lost to the plough all over the Wolds and they are now only visible on aerial photographs as shadowy marks in the soil or crop (*20*). The lines of trackways winding through the landscape that had been used for centuries were often scrubbed out and ploughed into the new fields. The boundaries of the old open fields had frequently been marked by earthen banks that sometimes dated to the Bronze Age and these were also erased. The new boundaries were made with quickset hawthorn hedges so that they did not use up too much of the valuable land. The impact of enclosure was so radical here that there are few ancient features visible on the surface of this landscape: Most of what we can see today dates from the eighteenth or nineteenth century.

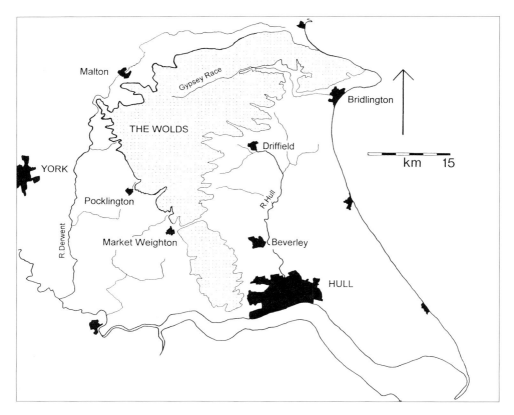

3 East Yorkshire and the Wolds. The main towns are concentrated around the wold-edge and the coast. The steep scarp slopes on the northern and western edge are marked with a bold line. The edge of the Wolds is depicted by the 60m contour

SOURCES AND APPROACHES

Given the radical changes of this period, how do we manage to see beyond them and investigate the character of this landscape as it was before 1700? There are few signs on the ground. It is rare to find preserved the track of a medieval routeway in scrubland on the edge of a set of enclosure fields or the earthen bank of a township boundary beneath an enclosure-period hedge.

To overcome these problems, we have to turn to both documentary sources and archaeology. Clues to the nature of the past landscape may come from maps drawn up at the time of enclosure. They sometimes record the look of the landscapes before the changes took place and are often the earliest detailed source available. Another valuable source is the first series of Ordnance Survey maps, produced at 6in scale during the middle decades of the nineteenth century.

By this time, enclosure had taken place but these maps continued to record the line of tracks and boundaries that have often been ploughed away over the last 150 years. The maps were produced by consultation with local people and often contain a wealth of local field names. These names can sometimes tell us where the open fields stood, or where the medieval pastures could be found, for it was only decades since they had become redundant. The maps also record upstanding earthworks of barrows or land boundaries which no longer exist today. They provide a unique snapshot of the nineteenth-century landscape and are an undervalued source of landscape information.

There are very few maps available from before the eighteenth century but there is a wealth of information relating to land grants and charters. These tend to date from the period between the twelfth and fifteenth centuries and record the giving of land to religious houses at places like Meaux Abbey and Bridlington Priory. Much of the high chalkland of the Wolds was granted in this way and each time a parcel of land changed hands, it is described and named along with the various rights of pasture or tillage associated with it. The earliest documentary record is Domesday Book produced in 1086.

It is a huge task to reconstruct the look and feel of the landscape in the past and the changes it went through. This involves not only mapping the layout of settlements, field boundaries and tracks but also trying to understand the manner in which human groups inhabited this area. Too often, historians and archaeologists take a restricted view focusing on a particular site or period. Most archaeologists would say that they specialise in a particular period or type of material (pottery, flint, plant remains) and their work is therefore highly focused. It is rare to find an historian who is equally at home with documentary research and archaeological fieldwork. As a result, there are very few broad studies that deal with specific regions using both historical and archaeological sources. It is even less common to find studies that transcend the divide between prehistory and the historical periods. Detailed, focused studies are very valuable but if we are to gain a wider picture of regional landscape change over the long term, we will have to cast the net much wider and use every available source from many different time periods.

The different communities that inhabited the Wolds between 1000 BC and AD 1500 would have had much in common. They would all have had an intimate awareness of the local landscape: the valleys, watercourses and viewpoints, as well as a boundless knowledge of local soils, water availability, animal and plant life. They also would have been aware of the relics of the past that littered much of this landscape, and no doubt, stories would have been told about barrows and names given to stretches of linear bank and ditch. Each generation would have had much in common with their ancestors who had farmed and inhabited the land many centuries earlier. If we are to get under the skin of this landscape and its changes, we need to look at it from a local perspective to familiarise ourselves with each place and try and picture what it would have been like in each period. This requires us to use as many sources as possible and trace the long-term changes within the same small area. Some of the landscape features such as boundary banks and trackways were used for very long periods of time and they serve as a link between periods separated by many centuries.

CHALK, DRY VALLEYS AND MERES

The Wolds landscape has a different feel to it than the surrounding lowlands. This is hard to pin down precisely but reflects a combination of its history, geology and current land-use. There have not been many trees or patches of woodland for many centuries. Even the eleventh-century Domesday Book records very little woodland on the Wolds compared to the vales of Holderness and York to the east and west. The only woodland today belongs to plantations created at the time of enclosure, often surrounding new farmhouses of the period. The hawthorn hedges are low and straight and there are very few other trees except for the occasional isolated ash with gnarled boughs starkly silhouetted against the sky (4). Coupled with the straight, wide roads and the bare rectangular fields, this gives the landscape an ordered appearance.

The land slopes gradually from west to east so that views are often long and wide (67). On a cold grey winter's day the openness can lend the place a bleak and windswept feel. However, at harvest time it is exhilarating to look out over a busy patchwork of orange and red fields. With a covering of snow, the orderly pattern of fields and roads is as prominent as dark grid lines against a white backdrop (5). At these times the landscape is like a map. It reveals the long history of the place as some of the meandering lines of bushy hedges belong to a much more ancient time than the eighteenth-century enclosure boundaries.

Geologically, the Wolds is made of chalk. It is a huge slab of hard white chalk tilted at a slight angle and sloping from west to east (3). At the eastern side, the chalk is overlain with deposits of clay which continue to the east coast, forming the flat lands of Holderness. In the west, the chalk sticks up above the vale of York and Pickering as a towering scarp. This provides the basis for the dramatic views over the vale of York from Arras or Garrowby Hill.

This topography clearly defines the edges of the Wolds to the west and north but on the eastern side, the chalk gradually slopes down into the clayland and its edge is not so obvious (*colour plates 3* and *4*). The difference between the western and eastern Wolds is defined not only by the scarp but also by the dry valleys that

4 A mature ash tree at Rabbit Dale, Huggate. Trees like this are often found in the grassland of the dry valleys

5 Looking north over Aunham Dale, Huggate. The regular outlines of the enclosure period fields and roads stand out against the snowy backdrop.

meander through the chalky bulk. These are steep sided V-shaped valleys, also known as dales or slacks, and they wind through the chalkland usually running from west or north-west to east or south-east. They were formed initially by fast-flowing streams that emerged out of melting glaciers but they no longer carry running water. Instead, they provide a series of dramatic sunken routes through the Wolds, each valley gradually broadening out towards the east (*colour plate 1*). The system resembles that of a mighty river, which begins in the west as a host of tiny streams running along steep gorges and gradually feeding into one another (*6* and *7*). As the valleys extend to the east and west of the watershed they become broader and less steep-sided until, on the eastern dip slope, the few valleys are wide with rolling sides almost indistinguishable from the rest of the landscape (*12*). This change is dramatic, often occurring over a distance of as little as 10km.

Today, the Wolds is a dry place with only one running stream. This is the Gypsey Race that runs from Duggleby Howe in the west along the base of its broad valley to Burton Fleming and beyond to Rudston, where it meets the North Sea at Bridlington (*3*). This stream is seasonal and is becoming less and less abundant as the demands of the water supply for surrounding towns drains the Derwent and forces the water table in the chalk of the Wolds to drop.

6 The steep slopes of Horse Dale cut through the rolling Wolds. A distant view of a dry valley

7 The valley of Millington Dale on the western edge of the Wolds

The stream and its valley, The Great Wold Valley, are pivotal features of the ancient Wolds landscape. A series of important Neolithic and Bronze Age monuments were situated along it clearly showing the symbolic role played by the stream in the minds of prehistoric communities. The complex of cursus monuments at Rudston are unique in Neolithic Britain and were laid out where the valley turns eastward to the sea. Here too stands the largest single standing stone in the country, probably first erected in the early Bronze Age.

Elsewhere on the Wolds, there are historical hints that streams did run in the last century but these were intermittent and occasional watercourses. They have all but disappeared as the water table has dropped since the mid-nineteenth century. The main sources of surface water are the numerous springs that erupt out of the chalk around the western, eastern and northern edges of the Wolds. These springs form the sources for the streams that run through the villages strung out along the base of the western escarpment such as Millington, Londesborough and Nunburnholme.

On the Wolds proper, there are no springs or streams as the chalk is porous and allows water to seep through to settle in the underground aquifer. Here, each village had its own pond or mere (*8* and *9*). These are usually found in the centre of the village surrounded by trees and often populated by ducks or

8 The pond at Fimber. There were two meres here until the nineteenth century. The village was named after them and they must have been important features of the prehistoric and historic landscape

geese. The meres were the only source of water for the medieval communities as very few wells were sunk. In some cases, there were two, side by side, as at Fridaythorpe and Fimber, where one was for human use and the other reserved for animals. The villages of Fimber and Sledmere are named after their meres and because these names are Old English in origin, the meres must be at least seventh-century in date (*colour plate 30*). The reliance of each village upon their mere is illustrated by a story that J.R. Mortimer recalled from his boyhood in Fimber. The young antiquarian remembered a battle fought with sticks and stones between the villagers of Fridaythorpe and Fimber over access to water during a very dry summer.

The origins of the meres are obscure but they may be natural occurrences where water collects in pockets of clay overlying the chalk. If so, they would also have been present in prehistory and would have impacted on the disposition of settlement in this period. There are some meres that are fed by springs, as at Burdale but this does not lie within a village (*26*).

THE STUDY AREA

The Wolds is a big place and we cannot begin to cover each part in as much detail as the next. Much of the discussion will deal with the area as a whole but at times it will be necessary to look more closely at a particular village, valley or even a single field or boundary. The majority of these local details will be drawn from the central part of the Wolds; an area between Driffield in the east and Pocklington in the west. This is a swathe of land that straddles the chalk and includes at least 22 townships. It is a varied land from the high Wold of Huggate and Fimber to the rolling countryside of Garton and North Dalton on the eastern dip slope (*9*). The medieval villages of Southburn, Eastburn and Kirkburn lay on the eastern edge of the Wolds where a series of springs emerge from the chalk to form the headwaters of the River Hull. Today, Southburn is a small hamlet whilst Eastburn has been depopulated. To the north-east is the town of Driffield, known today for its army barracks, but an important market for grain in the nineteenth century (*3*).

The study area includes the village of Sledmere which has a recent history very different to the rest of the 18 villages. It is the home of the Sykes family who owned much of this land in the late eighteenth and nineteenth centuries (*59*). They redesigned the village, moving its inhabitants to make room for a lavish landscape park and stately home. Their presence is still very much in evidence as the road through the village today is lined by stone memorials and follies built by successive generations of Sykes since the mid-eighteenth century.

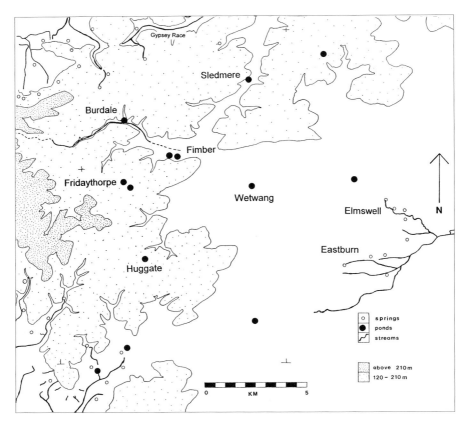

9 Water sources on the central Wolds. Most of this area is served only by meres, which are now situated in the middle of villages. Many of these could be natural water sources. In the nineteenth century there was an intermittent stream running between Burdale and Fimber, but this has not survived the fall in water table. The headwater springs of the Hull Valley emerge at the base of the eastern dip slope at Eastburn and Elmswell

The nearby village of Fimber is one of the smallest on the Wolds with a cluster of Victorian and Edwardian houses nestled around the pond, green and church. Commissioned by the Sykes, the church is Victorian in date and built on top of a Bronze Age barrow. That this spot has long been revered is evident in the traces of an eleventh-century church here as well as a possible earlier structure. In the Anglo-Saxon period the mound was used for burial. This practice of using prehistoric monuments as places of burial in later centuries is common on the Wolds and shows how the people living and working here were very conscious of the traces of the past that surrounded them. The long-term history of each place in this landscape is told through its past. The same places were returned to by people time and time again, the same tracks used but often in slightly different ways.

ARCHAEOLOGY ON THE WOLDS

We need to use disparate sources from many different time periods in order to tell the story of the changing landscape. Most of the work done by archaeologists and historians is more restricted than this but we can use the results of these detailed studies and weave them into the bigger picture. The Yorkshire Wolds as a whole is well known for its archaeological sites (*11*). A recent publication by the Royal Commission on the Historical Monuments of England, now part of English Heritage, has mapped the traces of cropmarks on aerial photographs (*20* and *32*). They show the course of ploughed-out ditches in fields of arable crops. The light chalky soil and the large amount of arable on the Wolds mean that this area responds well to aerial survey. The ditches, enclosures and trackways shown on the maps cannot be seen from ground level and are only visible from the air as on the surface they have been levelled by centuries of ploughing. The RCHM plots present a bewildering picture as they contain evidence from at least five millennia of settlement and farming activity (*27* and *33*). It is a difficult task to disentangle this jumble of enclosures, trackways, boundaries and barrows as most of them are undated.

Archaeological research on the Wolds largely began during the nineteenth century because of two local men. One was a vicar, Reverend E. Maule Cole of Wetwang and the other a corn merchant, J.R. Mortimer of Driffield. Mortimer's work was prolific and remains the most well known. In 1905, he produced a massive and detailed account, *Forty years researches into British and Saxon burial mounds on the Yorkshire Wolds* (*10*). He had excavated many Bronze Age barrows and, unlike his contemporaries, had meticulously recorded his findings with detailed description and drawings produced by his daughter, Agnes. Cole carried out few excavations but nonetheless produced a string of invaluable and insightful reports on diverse subjects including the geology of the dry valleys, water sources, Roman roads and prehistoric linear earthworks. It was Mortimer's collection of artefacts that formed the basis for the archaeology collections of the Hull and East Riding Museum and their continued exhibition is testament to the foresight of both Mortimer and the museum's early curator, Thomas Sheppard. In his 1911 obituary to Mortimer, Sheppard wrote:

> Probably no one in England has done so much for the elucidation of the prehistoric antiquities of his district as has Mr. Mortimer. No one has worked so well, so thoroughly, and so exhaustively; and certainly no one has so carefully preserved the records that were obtained. Unquestionably Mr. Mortimer's worth will be much more appreciated in the future even than it is today. Few, very few, yet realise the extreme value and importance of his collections.

10 J.R. Mortimer, the father of Wolds archaeology. *From Sheppard* 1911

Throughout the twentieth century, a number of important projects have shaped the way we now look at the archaeology of the Wolds (*11*). They have raised key issues regarding the long-term settlement of this landscape. Dominic Powlesland's excavations at Heslerton revealed the remains of an Anglo-Saxon settlement with rectangular post-built halls and an adjacent cemetery. There was evidence for a thriving rural economy spread over 20 hectares. The cemetery provided further data for the populations living and dying here and this project has contributed enormously to our knowledge of Anglo-Saxon settlement and society. The site lies beneath the northern escarpment of the Wolds on the southern edge of the vale of Pickering. A string of medieval villages are also found occupying this favourable location between the dry chalk Wolds and the marshy lowlands of the vale. Different types of land are accessible from this location and would have provided the settlement with a wide range of farming and food gathering opportunities.

Excavations at Wetwang and Garton Slack began in the 1970s after rich finds were located during quarrying works for gravel (*23,24* and *25*). The broad valley is filled with deep gravel deposits overlying the chalk and because these soils are not very good at showing up cropmarks the archaeological discoveries were largely unexpected. Over the last 25 years, a wide range of prehistoric and Roman finds have been found here but the site was made famous by the discovery of Iron Age cart burials in the early 1980s. Perhaps, more significant for understanding the nature of the Iron Age and Roman landscape was the discovery of a complete Iron Age cemetery and its adjacent settlement. The settlement was active throughout the Iron Age but continued into the Roman period after the cemetery had been abandoned. The site has given us a unique picture of the ways in which a settlement site evolved over several centuries. On many occasions new ditches were dug to enclose land and new settlements laid out, sometimes over the top of earlier graves.

Wharram Percy is one of the most well-known archaeological sites and projects in the country (*colour plates 10* and *11*). The excavations here began as an investigation of the phenomenon of village desertion in the late Middle Ages. Maurice Beresford and John Hurst wanted to know why so many sites had been abandoned between the fourteenth and sixteenth centuries and pioneered the use of archaeological techniques to try and answer such questions. Previously, these questions had been addressed purely through historical sources. Their fieldwork lasted forty years and the results have taken landscape studies much further than originally thought possible. Principally, they have shown that the site was occupied from as early as the Iron Age when some of the main tracks and boundaries were laid out. The site was settled in the Roman and Anglo-Saxon periods but in very different ways. There are hints that the medieval village originated as a planned settlement either side of the Norman Conquest although the precise dating is uncertain. Following the excavations, there has been fieldwork throughout the parish of Wharram Percy to try and build up a wider picture of the landscape surrounding the settlement. This has made it possible to trace the changing pattern of settlement here between the Roman period and the Middle Ages.

These three major projects at Heslerton, Wetwang-Garton Slack and Wharram Percy, dealing with different periods, have added enormously to our knowledge of the way that the Wolds was occupied between 1000 BC and AD 1500. It would be impossible to subject every township or valley to similar detailed scrutiny so we are left with the question of how the rest of the Wolds was settled. Can the picture at these three sites be transferred across this region? Where was settlement concentrated and what did the landscape look like? How was the Wolds farmed and by whom?

It has always been felt by archaeologists working here since the days of Mortimer that the chalk Wolds were favourable to ancient settlement. The light

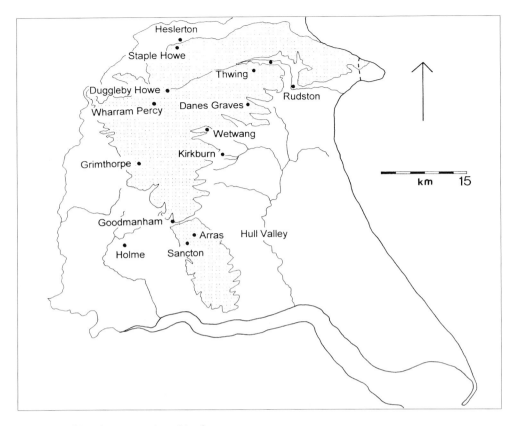

11 Archaeological sites mentioned in the text

soils made good and ready tillage and were also ideal as dry pasture. In contrast, the clay soils of the surrounding lowlands were considered too heavy for ancient plough technology. The Wolds contained a vast number of archaeological sites compared to the vales of Pickering and York and the plain of Holderness. It was therefore assumed that, during prehistory, the Wolds had been densely occupied and people had tended to avoid the low-lying vales. However, despite the large number of burial monuments there are very few known settlement sites before the Middle Ages. It was often argued that the domestic buildings of prehistoric communities were just too flimsy to identify and if they had existed on the Wolds they would have been ploughed away by centuries of arable agriculture. There was an assumption that people lived close to the graves of their ancestors and so the density of Iron Age cemeteries was taken to reflect the density of settlements. This is a familiar concept for us as it recalls the traditional picture of village, church and cemetery.

The discoveries at Heslerton and Wetwang seemed to confirm this view that the settlements did sit alongside their cemeteries both during the Iron Age and Anglo-Saxon period. One of the main aims of this book is to challenge these assumptions and especially the view that the Wolds was occupied and settled continuously between the Iron Age period and the Middle Ages. We will see that the real picture may be more complicated. Certainly, there were periods when the Wolds was farmed and settled on the same scale as the lowlands but equally there are others when it was largely uninhabited. At these times, it was used as pasture ground and for burial, but rarely for permanent settlement.

LONG-TERM HISTORY

Archaeologists have often treated the prehistoric past in the same way as a museum collection of finds by dividing it up into separate periods, each one divorced and different from the next. The division of prehistory into Neolithic, Bronze Age and Iron Age is based on objects and the way that technologies for making artefacts changed between 4000 BC and the Roman Conquest. Although all archaeologists are aware that these periods and their time boundaries do not apply or make sense on the ground, they are still used. The burial practices of the early Bronze Age (c.2300 BC-1700 BC) had more in common with the late Neolithic than they did with the middle or later Bronze Age. In fact, there was a real change in the middle of the Bronze Age (c.1500 BC) when burial monuments such as barrows ceased to be constructed. People began instead to spend time and effort on constructing land boundaries, field divisions and settlements. The Bronze Age itself is only held together by the common use of bronze and this did not dictate the look of the landscape or the nature of society. Whilst we will use these terms in this book, it must be stressed that they are simply convenient labels for slices of time and not as ways of explaining social change. The people living on the Wolds in 1000 BC would not have known that the Bronze Age was about to come to an end. In fact, many would have had little direct contact with the metal.

Once the study of the landscape extends into the Roman and Medieval periods the same criticisms apply. According to the traditional sequence we are expected to believe that everything changed at the Roman Conquest in AD 70, the date for the Conquest of East Yorkshire, and changed again in AD 410 when the Roman occupation is supposed to have officially come to an end. These are simply dates of political events as chronicled in the written histories. They have very little direct influence on the ground. In fact, we will see that alterations in the landscape seem to have taken place at different times than the expected historical thresholds.

The long-term changes in the landscape are not best explained through the codified sequence of Neolithic, Bronze Age, Iron Age and Roman period. The key to understanding change in the landscape lies in understanding the relationship that people had with the past and with their surroundings. In a prehistoric context where there were no written histories – the understanding of life and the world would have revolved around stories and songs. These would have been set in the landscape that was familiar to each community and their subject matter would have been the mythical past of that community and its ancestors. In this way, the landscape would have been filled with pieces of mythology and history known to each member.

The long-term history forces us to think outside the box. It means we can see the slow, unfolding progress of change but also be able to identify things that remain the same and marvel at their endurance. The value of the long-term study is that it forces us to consider the way that the past was perceived by these communities. As the landscape changed, there were elements of it that were woven into the new schemes so that changes become involved with the past. This is how history was written; constantly changing. Each community's understanding of history was not based on the facts of the past or what actually happened but on the needs and perceptions of the society in the present.

THE FORGOTTEN LANDSCAPES OF THE YORKSHIRE WOLDS

The purpose of this book is to discover the forgotten landscapes of the Wolds. We know about the grassland wastes of the seventeenth and early eighteenth century, the sheepwalks and abandoned villages. But there were also other periods when the chalklands were even more remote and removed from the inhabited heartlands of the lowlands and wold-edge. This aspect of the heritage of the place has been overlooked by archaeologists and historians. The chapters in the book are organised chronologically so that the story unfolds with time. I spend more time and energy on the periods when the open pastoral character of the Wolds was present (middle Iron Age, c. 500 BC to c. 100 BC, and Anglo-Saxon, c. AD 500 to c. AD 900). This evidence needs to be carefully presented for these ideas are not universally accepted.

Chapter two deals with the linear earthworks and the laying out of long distance boundaries at the beginning of the first millennium BC. They formed the framework for subsequent phases of land division and many of these monuments survived for thousands of years. Chapter three looks at the pastoral landscapes of the middle Iron Age, arguing that the Wolds was used for burial and grazing until the second or first century BC when it was colonised and occupied. Chapter four traces the development of the Romano-British landscape, focusing on the changes to settlement and agriculture during the third century AD. Chapters five and six look at issues surrounding the post-Roman period between the fifth and eleventh centuries AD. Chapter five presents some of the problems regarding settlement patterns during this time. In chapter six we look in detail at the documentary evidence for an open pastoral landscape between the sixth and ninth centuries AD. Chapter seven looks at the changes to this landscape in the centuries surrounding the Norman Conquest and then tells the story of the medieval and post medieval periods. In chapter eight we step back from these period-based narratives and take a more distant long-term view. The survival of certain places over many centuries is discussed. The development of this landscape unfolded as a series of rhythmic cycles, whereby the phases of open pasture were repeatedly replaced by periods of intensive arable cultivation and settlement. The chapter ends with a look at the nature of the Wolds today, as seen by the people who live there.

TWO

THE EARLIEST BOUNDARIES AT THE BEGINNING OF THE FIRST MILLENNIUM BC

Certain parts of England have always been well known for their archaeology. The chalk downs of southern England feature prominently in discussions of prehistoric society, mainly because of its large number of prehistoric monuments. Here, recent land use history has favoured their survival but the builders of monuments and diggers of ditches in prehistory do appear to have favoured certain areas. The Yorkshire Wolds serve a similar role for the north of England and boast a greater density of prehistoric sites than any other comparable area in the north. The Wolds monuments have suffered from plough damage over the last 150 years but many still survive as upstanding earthworks (*13*).

A massive system of linear ditches, locally known as dykes or entrenchments, runs right across the Wolds. Most are now flattened into the arable soil but when they were first constructed these linear earthworks were huge (*12, 15* and *16*). The ditches alone can be as deep as 2m with the upcast chalk spread out alongside to form a bank. Many of the dykes run for several miles across the landscape and most are made up of at least two parallel rows of ditch and bank. In some cases, there can be up to five or six parallel ditches. This is a perplexing and mysterious group of monuments, which cannot be easily explained. They appear to have acted as land boundaries but if so, they organised this landscape on a huge scale, dividing and enclosing whole swathes of countryside. The meandering course of the ditches closely follows the route of the dry valleys (*12*). Many ditches were cut into the steep sides of the dales just below the brow, whilst others strike out boldly across the rolling landscape on the wold tops.

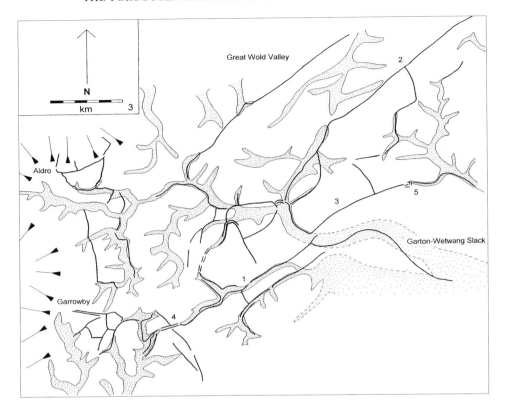

The construction of these monuments would have required large numbers of people digging the ditches with nothing more than tools of wood or bone, raising the spoil onto banks with wicker baskets or bags made of hide. Why were they created on such a massive scale? If they did act as boundaries, why was there a need for such an extensive system of land division? Why did the linears follow the lines of valleys so closely and did they relate to other features of the landscape?

There are some archaeological clues to date the linears but by no means enough to fully answer the questions of when they were built or whether they were all built at the same time. We know that many were constructed at the beginning of the first millennium BC at the end of the Bronze Age. They were so bulky and immovable that, once laid down, they continued to be used as boundaries and roadways throughout later prehistory and on into the Roman, Anglo-Saxon and medieval periods. Several linear earthworks were used as township and parish boundaries, others became reused as headlands in the medieval open fields and in some cases today can still be seen beneath hedge lines and field boundaries.

In this chapter, we consider some of the problems presented by these enigmatic

Opposite: 12 Linear earthworks and dry valleys in the central Wolds. The close relationship between the linears and the topography is apparent: 1. Middleham Dale; 2. Great Wold Dyke; 3. Green Lane; 4. Huggate Dykes; 5. Warren Dale. *Based on Mortimer 1905 and Stoertz 1997*

Right: 13 Willy Howe. Round barrows like this one were ubiquitous features of the late prehistoric and historic landscape

monuments, especially the part they play in dividing the landscape at the end of the Bronze Age (*c*.1000–800 BC). It was at this time that the Wolds was first divided and enclosed. Until then, prehistoric communities had probably used the area for pasture and burial. It was still full of the barrows that were thrown up to cover the graves of the dead during the late Neolithic and earlier part of the Bronze Age (2500–1800 BC) (*13*). At this time the land was probably not directly controlled or owned by specific households or families but instead may have been held in common amongst a large community. The question of how the land was owned, controlled, used and divided is crucial to the history of the Wolds landscape and it is these first ditched boundaries that set the scene for the developments of later centuries.

FRANCIS DRAKE, THE VICAR AND THE CORN MERCHANT

We owe a great deal to the pioneering antiquarians who began to investigate the barrows and earthworks of rural Britain in the eighteenth and nineteenth

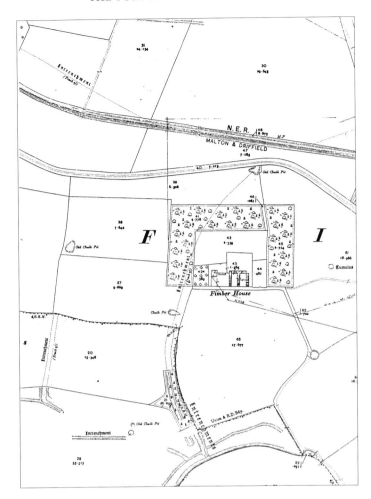

14 The linear earthworks at Fimber Westfield as they were in 1910. The upstanding earthworks are visible at the bottom of the picture. They originally ran northwards through the two chalk pits. *Ordnance survey 1910 25 inch series*

centuries. All over the country, inquisitive Victorians started to realise that they could discover the past, not only through the written word in dusty documents but also by recovering objects from the ground. In doing so, they were creating the archaeology that we know today. This disparate band of knowledgeable and resourceful men, for they were mostly male, began to develop the fieldwork skills that became the foundations for modern archaeology. The artefacts they discovered formed the collections that filled the shelves of our regional museums and kick-started the careful and meticulous study of artefacts that would itself form the basis for the way we divide up prehistory into periods. Without such physical investigations, we could not begin to understand the prehistoric communities of Britain and the ways in which they lived, worked and died.

1 The dry valley at Sylvan Dale, Millington

2 Walkers' routes near Londesbrough

3 A view from the scarp slope above Bishop Wilton on the western wold-edge

4 Looking north over the Vale of Pickering from the scarp slope above West Heslerton

5 Access to the Sledmere Estate is permitted, but controlled

6 Estate workers' houses in Sledmere village

7 The village of West Heslerton at the base of the escarpment on the northern wold-edge

8 The post bus reaches out to remote rural communities

9 The estate village at Warter

10 The ruined church and pond at Wharram Percy

11 Looking out towards the graveyard at Wharram Percy

12 Primroses in Millington Pastures

13 Gorse bush in Sylvan Dale

14 Hawthorn hedge near Nunburnholme

15 Buttercups in Millington Pastures

16 Poppies near Bracie Bridge

17 Round barrow on Garrowby Hill

18 Warter church

19 Fields of rapeseed

20 The Sykes monument

21 The footpath leading out from the end of Tibthorpe Green Lane now diverted around the edge of enclosure period fields

22 The end of the Tibthorpe Green Lane looking west

23 The Sledmere Green Lane looking west towards the Sykes monument

24 Huggate Dykes earthworks showing a single ditch running off to the left of picture along the top of the dale side

25 Multiple banks of earthworks at Huggate Dykes

26 The head of the dry valley at Horse Dale, looking north towards Fridaythorpe

27 Looking west from the scarp slope above Nunburnholme towards the Vale of York

28 Aerial view of excavations at Melton alongside the A63 to Hull. The ditched trackway running from left to right is the east–west track mentioned in the text and dates to the late Iron Age. *Courtesy Derek Brooks*

29 Two of the main boundary ditches at Melton with a line of pits or postholes flanking one of the ditches. The date of these boundaries is unclear but they were both probably laid out during the middle or later Iron Age. *Courtesy On-site Archaeology*

30 Looking south-east over Fimber pond

31 The majority of the Wolds is now under intensive arable cultivation

32 and 33 Archaeological excavations in progress

In East Yorkshire, the Wolds captured the attention and imagination of these historical frontiersmen. It was here that many burial mounds or barrows were preserved in grassy pastures or field corners as upstanding earthworks (*13* and *colour plate 17*). They became an easy target for the antiquarians, who soon realised that they had been used for burial and often contained the remains of the dead along with accompanying grave goods of flint, pottery and sometimes bronze. There is no doubt that many barrow diggers plundered the relics for their novelty or monetary value without making a record. However, a few antiquarians recognised the historical importance of the remains and took time to carefully record and publish their findings.

J.R. Mortimer was born in the village of Fimber and was brought up at Leavening on the western edge of the Wolds (*10*). He ran a corn merchant's business in Driffield but was better known as an avid antiquarian. During much of the second half of the nineteenth century, he excavated hundreds of barrows on the central Wolds and published his work in 1905 in the seminal work for East Yorkshire archaeology, *Forty Years Researches in British and Saxon Burial Mounds of East Yorkshire*. In addition to the barrows, he looked at the enigmatic linear earthworks that could be seen stretching for miles across the Wolds.

Mortimer may have left us a unique and valuable document of his excavations but he was not alone in trying to understand these monuments. The linear earthworks were already being discussed and studied as early as the middle of the eighteenth century. At this time, there was very little appreciation of prehistory and most people's understanding of the past came from a classically based education. The banks and ditches of the linear earthworks first appeared in print in a discussion of the history of Roman Britain and the search for the lost Roman town of *Delgovitia*. A paper by Francis Drake dated 1747 puts forward a series of locations for the Roman settlement which is known from historical sources to lie between the Roman towns of York, Malton and Brough. In doing so, he remarked upon the massive entrenchments to be found around Garrowby Hill on the top of the western escarpment of the Wolds:

> On top of this mountain, though the road turns up it by an easy ascent, begins a series of such enormous works for fortification, as the like is not to be met with in the whole island.

He continued associating the earthworks with Roman defensive works:

> To the southwest, there are no ramparts thrown up; but to the east, northeast and due north, the whole country is full of them. The vales are all guarded by small encampments at their angles; the vestiges of barracks, now visible, are called by

the country people the camps. These were to prevent any sudden surprise that way. On the hills, from vale to vale, some of which are from 60 to 90 yards deep, and prodigiously steep, are thrown up works, as ramparts, 12 yards broad, and proportionably high, which join in right angles with the vallies and serve as a strong barrier everywhere.

The earthworks were far better preserved in 1747 than they are today. Around the same time, Haynes produced a map of this area and it too records the line of entrenchments around the villages of Huggate, Fridaythorpe and Millington.

A hundred years later, the interpretation of the linear earthworks had developed and they were no longer seen as Roman military works. By this time people had begun to realise that the prehistoric communities of Britain were not simply 'barbaric savages' who got in the way of the might of Roman civilisation but possessed their own distinctive cultural and social characteristics. J.R. Mortimer devoted a whole section in his book to the study of the linear earthworks and this included the results of numerous excavations as well as some discussion of their date and function. He produced a fine map covering a broad swathe of the central Wolds on which he plotted the course of miles of banks and ditches (12). E. Maule-Cole, the vicar of Wetwang, produced a similar map and published his thoughts on the prehistory and archaeology of the area.

Other notable contributors to the debate at the time were Mortimer's brother, Robert, who created a very detailed map of the area around Fimber (1886); Charles Newton who put his name to the Map of British and Roman Yorkshire in 1846; and Major General Pitt Rivers who carried out excavations on the massive earthwork of Danes Dyke on Flamborough Head. Each one had their own thoughts and ideas about the role that these enormous linear banks and ditches had played in the past. Pitt Rivers considered that they formed part of an extensive defensive system constructed by an invading force, which was proceeding inland after embarking on the east coast. Mortimer disagreed with Pitt Rivers that the dykes had been built for defensive purposes instead arguing that they represented the territorial boundaries of a settled community. Mortimer wrote:

> They would, in many cases, serve as enclosures for family or even tribal boundaries and tribal settlements, and were admirably adapted for keeping cattle.

He did recognise a defensive role for some of the ditches that ran along the steep dale sides (*colour plate 24*). He argued that these were deep enough to have acted as concealed ways hiding the traveller from view either from the dale bottom or open ground above.

15 Huggate Dykes is one of the few examples where these earthworks remain upstanding. In the nineteenth century these banks continued into the field beyond but have since been ploughed up

The flintworking waste found within the bank of Danes Dyke suggested a prehistoric date for its construction. All of these early archaeologists agreed that the linears, were later than the early Bronze Age round barrows but earlier than the Roman roads that sometimes cut through the banks and ditches. In some places, Mortimer had found Anglo-Saxon graves laid along the ditches of these monuments, which again pointed to a late prehistoric or Roman date. Cole argued that they were prehistoric in date, posing the question in an article of 1888:

> Were the entrenchments of the Wolds the work of the Britons or of the Romans? I have no hesitation in saying of the former; for one reason, and that is a good one, that there is not a straight line amongst the whole lot.

The writings of Mortimer and Cole both lament the loss of the earthworks, which were being ploughed away as farming became more intensive. The destruction to the banks, ditches and barrows had been hastened by the enclosure of the Wolds, which carried on throughout the nineteenth century and turned many tracts of rough grassland into arable fields. The following extract from Mortimer, describes the process but also shows how the two budding archaeologists could recognise marks in the ploughsoil for what they once represented:

Even since the writer was a boy, many of the entrenchments passing from hill to hill have been removed by the labours of the husbandmen, and many of the ramparts which then stood out in bold relief are now razed to a level with the natural surface of the land, with the ditches filled in; their former existence being now only traceable on the surface by the line of rubbly stone from the ploughed down ramparts, and the green bands in the growing corn caused by the additional depth of soil in the filled up ditches.

Another valuable record of the earthworks are the Ordnance Survey first edition 6in series maps for East Yorkshire, produced in the 1850s. They sought to record all ancient remains that were still visible in the landscape. Mortimer's personal copies of the 1854 maps are kept in the Hull Museum and are annotated with his sketches and remarks. More detailed maps were later produced at 25in scale and together both series are a valuable source for tracing the former course of the earthworks, which are now largely levelled under the plough (*14, 19* and *69*).

NEW LIGHT IN THE TWENTIETH CENTURY

Since Mortimer's day the vast majority of these earthworks have been levelled by the plough and today they rarely survive as upstanding monuments. However, archaeological techniques have come a long way. Through a combination of excavation, aerial photography and ground survey, it has been possible to map the distribution of these linear banks and ditches. In particular the use of aerial photography has revolutionised the way we can illustrate huge swathes of the ancient landscape (*20*). This technique is especially useful in an arable countryside such as the Yorkshire Wolds where the tracks of ploughed down ditches and banks can be photographed from the air and mapped (*27* and *33*).

The light chalky soils of the Wolds tend to show up these cropmarks and soilmarks very clearly and over the years a large number of photographs have been taken. This information was brought together by the Royal Commission on the Historical Monuments of England, now part of English Heritage, who plotted it onto a series of maps covering the whole of the Wolds. This volume is a valuable resource but is only the starting point, as many of the thousands of sites have not been dated and their functions remain unclear. Mortimer's record is as good as anything that has been produced in the twentieth century. There are some sites where short stretches of linear earthwork do still survive where the plough has not penetrated (*15*). The steep dale sides are often scoured by grassed over ditches and these can also be seen within plantations, woodland and shelter belts (*16* and *18*).

16 The multiple banks of Huggate Dykes looking down towards Tun Dale. This shows how the arrangement of ditches and banks here straddled the neck of land between the heads of two dry valleys

At the beginning of the twenty-first century, we know more about these mysterious banks and ditches than Mortimer did at the onset of the twentieth, but there is still a great deal to discover. The highlights of the twentieth century have been the few excavations across these monuments. From the excavations into the linear earthworks, we know that they were laid out at different times between about 1000 BC and AD 1000. Datable pottery, such as Late Bronze Age sherds from Thwing have been found at the bottom of the ditches, suggesting a date for their actual construction. We know that these ditches continued to fill up with sediment long after they were dug so many examples produce Roman-period pottery from the upper fills. This does not mean they were first excavated and used in the Roman period but that the ditches must have been in the process of silting up at this time.

Many stretches of bank and ditch remain undated but in some cases we can say that certain ditches were dug in the Iron Age or the Roman period. At Cowlam for instance, a length of ditch and bank was proven to be later than a small group of Iron-Age square barrows and so must date from any time after about 300 BC. Another ditch was investigated as part of the excavations at Wetwang Slack and shown through excavation to have been dug around the second century BC.

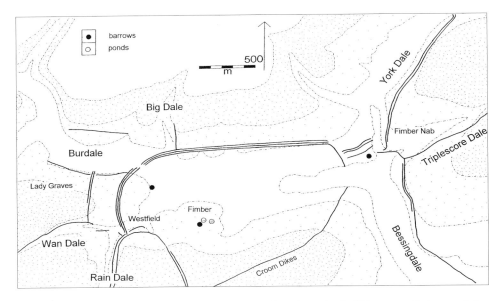

17 The Fimber area showing the layout of linear earthworks and relief. The great ditches tended to follow the lines of valleys and several converged at Fimber Nab. The area now occupied by the village, where the ponds are marked, was completely enclosed by linears

Other ditches have been filled with Roman pottery with little prehistoric material and these ditches were probably constructed in the Roman period. The digging of long distance ditched boundaries was not restricted to one period and was used for land division on the Wolds for over 2000 years (*23*).

Many areas of England have evidence of prehistoric field boundaries but very few possess the long-distance ditch and bank boundaries that occur on the Wolds. Elsewhere in the country, monumental ditches such as these were first constructed during the late Bronze Age between 1000 and 800 BC. A lot of work has been carried out on the linear earthworks of Salisbury Plain, another block of chalk downland and here the ditches were shown to have served as boundaries to territories based around late Bronze Age settlements. A similar date was given to linear earthworks on the Tabular Hills of North Yorkshire and to ditched boundaries on the Berkshire Downs.

The earliest linear ditches from the Wolds also date from the late Bronze Age. In several places pot sherds dating to around 900 or 800 BC have been found in the earliest fills of the ditches. In itself, this is not enough to give the ditches a late Bronze Age date as this pottery could have been disturbed from the ground surface when the ditch was dug. More conclusive evidence came from a length of bank and ditch at Fimber Westfield in the heart of the Wolds (*14* and *18*). Here,

Mortimer discovered a pit that had been cut into the bank of the earthwork and the pit had been filled with, 'curious pieces of burnt clay'. These were later identified as fragments of moulds for making bronze spearheads and could be dated between 1100 and 900 BC. As they were found within a pit that had been cut into the bank the moulds must be later than the earthwork. In another excavation during the 1950s, C. and E. Grantham, whose collection of artefacts formed the basis for a small private museum, excavated a stretch of linear ditch and bank close to the Sykes monument at Sledmere (70 and 71). They found several sherds of late Bronze Age pottery within the bank.

It would be foolish to say for sure that all the linear ditches were dug during the late Bronze Age as only a small number have been excavated and produced dating evidence. However, it is reasonable to suggest that there was a huge reorganisation of the landscape in this period that involved the digging of massive monumental long distance boundaries on the Wolds. The longest and largest earthworks do appear to date from this time and they seem to have laid the basis for the land division on the Wolds for hundreds, if not thousands, of years.

MOBILE TO ENCLOSED LANDSCAPES

The archaeological remains and landscapes from across Britain tell us that society was changing in many ways towards the end of the second millennium BC (1000 BC). Change must have occurred very gradually over several hundred years, but when we take a step back and look at the patterns across the second millennium BC, the distinction is stark. At the beginning of this millennium (2000 BC), the landscape on the Wolds and throughout much of Britain would have been populated by communities who did not inhabit permanent, fixed settlements. They would have been based in a number of temporary sites and perhaps moved from one to another according to seasonal or annual cycles. They buried their dead in graves beneath round earthen barrows, which became visible markers in the landscape. Thousands of years later, some of these barrows would still have been visible and have possessed enough meaning to be used as boundary markers or places of congregation. The landscapes of the early Bronze Age lacked obvious, fixed boundaries and it seems that land was not divided amongst separate groups but belonged to everyone and no one. Instead of boundaries, people who moved freely about the land used trackways to order and organise the landscape.

In many other areas of Britain, land boundaries and field patterns were laid out for the first time during the middle of the second millennium BC (1500 BC). At the same time, people stopped burying their dead in prominent barrows.

It would appear that their efforts were gradually diverted away from building ceremonial monuments and towards the construction of ditched boundaries and settlement enclosures. This distinction is a clear archaeological change and forces us to consider the way that society was changing, especially with regard to the way that landscapes were used and understood.

Both the settlements and the land boundaries demanded a huge amount of labour. Some of the ditches are 2m deep and stretch for up to 20km across the landscape (*12*). When we imagine the number of people required to dig these boundaries, we inevitably start to think about how the labour force was organised. Who were the labourers who did all the work? Were the boundaries laid out in a random fashion or did they follow lines that were already understood in the mobile landscape? Why were the ditches so monumental and massive? We do not have the answers to many of these questions, but need to keep asking them so that all possibilities are covered.

The Wolds landscape began to be divided at the end of the second millennium BC (1000 BC). At the same time, a group of settlements surrounded by deep ditches and banks were also constructed. In some cases, these sites, such as Thwing and Staple Howe, appear to relate to the pattern of linear ditches. They were new types of settlement and were often located at prominent places alongside the ditches or sometimes, at junctions of the linear boundaries. The construction and occupation of these enclosed settlements must have been initiated by the same communities and perhaps for the same reasons as the building of the linear boundaries. The way that these settlements were inhabited might tell us about the reasons behind the new land divisions.

LINEAR EARTHWORKS AROUND FIMBER

There is a political slogan, 'Think global … Act local', which sums up neatly the crucial role of the individual in the worldwide movement for environmental change. We can also apply this principle to archaeology. In order to address the big questions of how past societies were organised, it is important to look in detail at specific localities and individual sites. We will start by looking at the area around Fimber in the central Wolds.

This small, idyllic village sits on raised ground looking over the broad dry valley that runs past on its way to Thixendale (*8, 14, 17* and *19*). The old railway track from Malton to Driffield still runs along the valley bottom. This has been disused for decades but is now a haven for wildlife and walkers. The area around Fimber is full of the remains of linear earthworks but they are rarely visible on the ground. The landscape is arable and the relentless, deep ploughing of

18 The surviving ditch of one of the earthworks at Fimber Westfield

modern times has taken its toll on these monuments. In the nineteenth century, there were many stretches of bank and ditch still extant as earthworks. These were recorded by the Ordnance Survey in 1854 and again in 1910 on a 25in scale. Where the earthworks still survive, they correspond with their location on these maps, showing the skill and reliability of the Victorian surveyors. One extract from the 1910 map shows the line of an earthwork passing through two chalk pits (*14*). They must have been placed here to take advantage of the readily available supply of chalk blocks that formed part of the banks of the monument. Most of these earthworks can be dated back to the late Bronze Age and must have formed an indelible part of this landscape for many centuries. They had survived largely intact for nearly 3000 years until the twentieth century when intrusive farming methods razed them to the ground. Until this point, many generations of local people would have known the monuments. Some would have seen them as a hindrance to the smooth running of the farming landscape; others would have accepted their presence and worked around them whilst wondering about their antiquity and marvelling at their scale.

The massive linear passing by Fimber to the north was used as the edge of the open field around the village. To the west is a farm known today as Fimber Westfield, but in 1910 it was called Fimber House. The farm must have been built between 1854 and 1910, as it does not appear on the first edition OS maps. A few

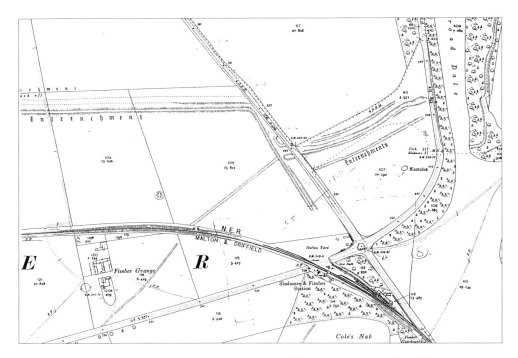

19 The earthworks at Fimber Nab as they were in 1910. The way they were followed by the township boundaries (dotted lines) can be clearly seen. The diagonal earthwork running along past Fimber Grange is the remains of the coach road that also ran along the north side of the earthworks. *Ordnance Survey 1910 25in series*

hundred metres south of this farmhouse there are some enormous earthworks preserved on the grassy dale sides. The bulky banks of chalk run directly down the slope and then disappear beneath the flat ground of the narrow valley bottom (*14* and *18*). Excavations here in the early 1980s showed that the earthwork had originally run down across the valley floor and up the other side where its banks are still visible. At the base of the valley, the hillwash dislodged from the valley sides by deforestation and Wold-top ploughing has gradually worked its way downslope to accumulate, slowly submerging the earthworks. These are some of the best preserved earthworks of their kind on the Wolds and it is clear from looking at the north facing dale side that they were not all constructed at the same time.

The largest earthwork was made up of four banks running down the slope with probably three intervening ditches (*14*). The excavations across these earthworks on the other side of the dale revealed the same number of ditches and banks, but showed that one of the ditches had begun life as a series of pits. One of the banks begins close to the top of the valley side, whilst the other three are not visible until halfway down the slope. The biggest bank overlies a ditch, which runs at 90° to the main earthwork along the upper slopes of the valley side, thus making its construction later (*17*). In several other places, the same relationship occurs where the single ditches running along the contour are overlain by larger banks.

This relationship was something that Mortimer recognised through excavation in a number of sites around Fimber. He suggested that the earlier single ditches may have acted as trackways following the valleys and converging on the site of the village whilst the later massive banks and ditches were designed to enclose this area. Parts of the large enclosing linear earthwork were definitely constructed before or during the later Bronze Age, which means that the single ditches that converge on the village site and its ponds may be earlier than that.

The major multiple earthwork does indeed enclose a large tract of land. It runs from Fimber Westfield northwards for 800m and then turns round gradually to the east stretching for 1.5km, until it reaches the junction of two valleys just before Fimber Nab (*17* and *19*). This piece of country is where two major valleys converge. Burdale comes in from the west and York Dale from the north and it is here that these two valleys combine to form Bessingdale, which runs southwards to eventually open out into Wetwang Slack. This is the place where the steep-sided dry valleys of the northern and western Wolds start to broaden out, their sides becoming less steep and their bases less narrow. A number of other smaller dry valleys also feed into the area and these too are embellished with linear earthworks.

There can be no doubt that the linear ditches and banks were laid out to follow the valleys but the reasons for this are obscure. Was it because these ridges and slopes were already being used to demarcate territory or were they simply convenient reference points for the new boundaries? Could these landforms have held other significances related to mythology or ancestors? Maybe it was important to capture these meanings by following the valley lines and mimicking the topography with the form of the banks and ditches.

The main multiple earthwork surrounds the village on its northern side where it is now only visible as soil marks in the ploughed fields. These are parallel lines of chalk defined also by the dark colour of the fills of the intervening ditches. An old road may have once followed the earthworks as the modern road into the village from the east is a late addition to the landscape, probably laid out in the eighteenth or nineteenth century. The banks and ditches were also followed by a hedge line and in places, the earthwork bank is still visible beneath the hedge (*19*).

When the valley changes direction, so too does the earthwork. Where York Dale heads off to Sledmere and the north, the earthwork changes character. Part of it veers off to the south whilst another series of massive banks and ditches run

for 300m across a spur of land. This promontory of Wold land, known locally as a 'nab', marks the edge of the southern end of York Dale but also faces to the south and Bessingdale (*17*). The edges of both valleys were followed by linear earthworks and these can be up to three banks wide, preserved above the ground within the plantations. A more modest single ditch runs along the side of the smaller valley, Triplescore Dale, that sits between the two major valleys.

The earthworks on the spur are now flattened into the field but in the nineteenth century, they stood to a considerable height. They could be seen from the train and were investigated on separate occasions by Thomas Wiltshire and J.R. Mortimer. Both antiquarians recorded that the banks were 1.5m high and the ditches were 2m deep. These are now only visible as cropmarks from the air but were recorded by the Ordnance Survey in 1854, 1899 and 1910 (*19*). Both antiquarians produced measured profiles of the earthworks. These drawings showed a series of ditches and banks and in one place, a level strip between one of the banks and its associated ditch. Mortimer refers to this flattened area as a *berm*, a defensive feature usually found amongst earthwork fortifications. Wiltshire's profile provides a more accurate view and his survey shows that it may have been caused by the use of the chalk bank as a roadway. We know that this section of earthwork did carry a coach road in the eighteenth century and it would make sense to use such a prominent, well-drained and solid mound of chalk for this purpose.

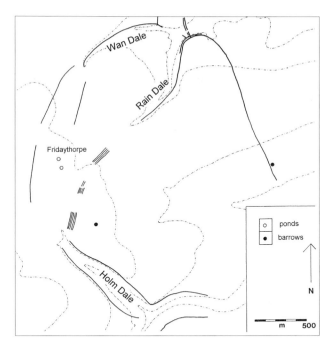

Opposite: 20 Aerial photograph of the head of Horse Dale showing cropmarks of multiple linear ditches running out from the valley head. See fig. 21 for map of same area. *Courtesy English Heritage Crown copyright*

Right: 21 Map showing the course of multiple banks and ditches to the south of Fridaythorpe. They connected the heads of these two dry valleys and helped to enclose the two ponds that now lie in the centre of the village

A number of important points regarding the layout of the linear ditches are illustrated by the Fimber area. The first is the way that the linears followed the lines of the valleys. This is straightforward and perhaps to be expected. In many places the linears ran along the ridges of the valleys and this might be explained as boundaries demarcating blocks of land that were already defined by the natural topography (*12*). The ditches were simply expressing the natural boundaries in a more permanent form. However, the form of the earthworks changed depending on the kind of topographic situation. For example, single ditches without banks are only found running along the upper slopes of minor dry valleys. Large long-distance linears are usually found running along open ridges and the largest and multiple systems of parallel ditches and banks are always found stretched across the necks of land between the heads of valleys (*20* and *21*). In this way the linear ditches do not simply follow the natural lines in the landscape, they actually change their form depending on what kind of topographic situation they find themselves in. Once we recognise this strong relationship between the linears and the lay of the land, we begin to realise that the physical form of the landscape must have been of crucial importance to the people who constructed these ditches and boundaries.

WHAT DID THE LANDSCAPE MEAN TO PEOPLE?

The purpose of archaeology is not simply to study pottery or to produce maps of field boundaries but to try and understand people, their lives and beliefs as well as their relationships with each other, the environment and their history. For too long, ancient landscapes were seen simply as areas of land that had been used for farming and settlement. The relationship between people and the landscape was simply explained as the battle for survival between prehistoric communities, the climate and the soil. This is important, but only part of the story. As anthropologists know, societies across the world live complex spiritual and social lives, which are not completely concerned with producing food or providing shelter. The way that people understood their surroundings is one example. The indigenous peoples of Australia are well known for transforming their landscapes into magical, mythical places where their ancestors abide. Mountains, streams and rocks are all named and each landscape feature plays its part in stories that relate the ancestral origins of living tribes and families. For these people, a journey along a trackway is not just about getting from A to B. It represents a spiritual journey into the mythical history of their ancestors, a means of travelling to another time or another world.

Ceremonial monuments dominated the landscapes of the Neolithic and early Bronze Age in Britain. Large earthen mounds were built in places that had long been used for burial and, in some places, huge ditched enclosures or processional avenues were constructed. These monuments were created to express what the landscape meant to the communities that lived there. They were often tied up with the burial of the dead and it is hard to escape the idea that the ancestral spirits continued to live on in these magical landscapes. Much more effort was put into building monuments than was given to making settlements or field boundaries between 4000 and 1800 BC. The significance and meaning given to places in the landscape must always have been complex and is difficult to understand. No doubt names were given to valleys, hilltops, springs and view points and in some cases these may have been associated with ancestors or mythical beings from more remote times. It is through the naming and storytelling that places became meaningful to people. In a society without written records, these stories and places became the way that the people remembered their history and preserved it by word of mouth from one generation to the next. The landscape soaked up the past and became full of memories, meanings, names and myths all entangled in the imagination of the young and the old. Ceremonial monuments were built in significant parts of the landscape, either at viewpoints, alongside trackways or boundaries or on the edge of pastures or fields.

Archaeologists have often stressed that during the second millennium BC the old ceremonial landscape dominated by monuments and trackways was gradually replaced with an agricultural landscape dominated by boundaries and settlements. This change is regularly described as a radical re-orientation of the meaning of the landscape, reflecting a change in the way communities thought about both their world and themselves. It brought with it a transformation in the way that the land was organised. The ceremonial landscape had revolved around places and paths whereas the agricultural landscape contained areas of land limited by fixed boundaries. These are the changes we are seeing when the linear earthworks were constructed.

The building of long-distance, linear ditches and their use as boundaries was a completely new way of making sense of the landscape. It would be easy to argue that this marked a break with the past, an end to a landscape of tracks and burial mounds and the beginning of a landscape of enclosure and farming. However, the builders of the linear ditches were well aware of the earlier markers and meanings and, in many cases, appear to have laid out the new boundaries with respect to the features of this earlier landscape. We have already seen how the linears related to the topography but there are also relationships with barrows, meres and trackways; all important markers in the landscapes of the Neolithic and early Bronze Age.

MERES, TRACKWAYS AND BARROWS

Mortimer recognised that many of the Wolds linears had cut through or otherwise respected the round barrows. He used this as a means of relatively dating the linears. He remarked that:

> When planning these earthworks it would seem that in many instances certain barrows had been chosen as points to mark the direction the entrenchments should take; hence the not infrequent collision of the two and the mutilation of the barrow.

In many parts of the Wolds some of the largest long-distance linears like the Great Wold Dyke seem to have used the barrows as markers. We know the date of the barrows and that the linear land boundaries began to be built 1000 years after them. It is easy to show that the layout of linears was designed with them in mind. The late Bronze Age linears of both Salisbury Plain and the Tabular Hills of North Yorkshire also often followed the barrows and it is accepted that the land units outlined by the boundaries were based on existing territorial patterns.

The meres had also been part of the mobile landscapes of the Bronze Age and these were also respected by the ditched boundaries of the late Bronze Age (*8* and *colour plate 30*). There are several cases where linear ditches were laid out to lead past the meres or in the case of Fimber and Fridaythorpe, enclose them (*17* and *21*). It is highly likely that these water sources were present in prehistory when they would have provided essential water supplies for roaming populations and their animals. Like the barrows, they would have been some of the most significant features of the landscape and it is no surprise that the layout of new boundaries took notice of them. This would most especially be the case if the new territories were designed for organising pasture grounds, as each pasture would need access to water sources. On the edge of the Wolds, there are places where the linears head directly for springs before stopping short. This may be related to the organising of access to the springs so that animals from both enclosed pastures could be watered from the same spring.

That the new system of boundaries was oriented around meres, springs and sometimes barrows is not in question. Another aspect of the earlier mobile landscape was a series of trackways that crossed the Wolds usually from west to east. Trackways are always difficult to date. They tend to survive in the landscape for long periods of time, sometimes over several centuries or even millennia. For this reason, it is hard for the archaeologist or landscape historian to work out when the trackways originated. They do not present the usual archaeological signatures that may be present in a barrow or even the datable pottery in the ditch of a boundary.

We can be fairly certain of the route of some of the more important routeways from this period. Some provide natural ways across the chalklands, taking account of the course of valleys and taking care to avoid the steepest slopes. Many of these tracks have a clear, long distance outlook as they strike boldly across the open landscape of the Wolds their attention fixed on the distant horizon rather than taking care to meander between local objectives (*22*).

There are two main candidates for long-distance early trackways and they have both survived into recent times. One runs from Aldro on the western edge of the Wolds through Sledmere and on towards Bridlington and Filey on the east coast. This we will call Towthorpe ridgeway. The other lies in parallel to the south. It begins at Garrowby Hill and heads eastwards, passing between Sledmere and Garton townships and on towards Rudston with its unique concentration of Neolithic and Bronze Age monuments. This latter trackway will feature heavily in the following pages as it survives in many different forms for over 4000 years. We will call it the Sledmere Green Lane. If these are long-distance tracks then they were well sited as they both line up with the raised and well drained gravel ridges or moraines that stretch across the Vale of York to the west. These two routes would have been the easiest ways to cross the low-lying, boggy ground of the vale. The tracks may no longer provide routeways across the Wolds, but stretches of them have been preserved as field boundaries, lanes and as boundaries

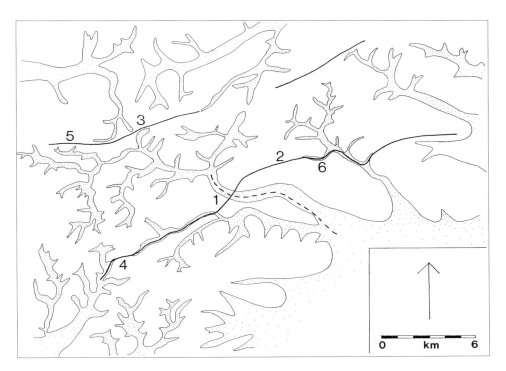

22 Possible prehistoric trackways across the Wolds that were followed by the linear ditched boundaries in the late Bronze Age: 1. Blealands Nook; 2. Green Lane; 3. Towthorpe Ridgeway; 4. Huggate Dykes; 5. Vessey pond; 6. Warren Dale

between medieval townships. Both tracks can be picked out on a modern map as continuous lines running across the page between the confusion of many centuries of change. Their routes also tend to follow the lines of the topography running along the lines of the winding valleys, as well as crossing the narrow necks of land between the valleys. They behave like the ridgeways of the South Downs and Wessex chalklands that follow the highest ground and ridges.

These routes would have been key features of the Bronze Age landscape and in fact the Towthorpe ridgeway is followed for some of its course by a string of barrows. This routeway may well originate before the Bronze Age, as fieldwalking picked up a high concentration of Neolithic and earlier flintworking waste around a backfilled pond close to the ridgeway at Vessey.

In some cases, the boundaries that were laid out at the end of the Bronze Age appear to have followed these tracks, just as they followed the valleys and used barrows and ponds as markers and alignment points. The Sledmere Green Lane for instance was followed by a series of three parallel banks and ditches for several kilometres as it passed by the villages of Wetwang, Fridaythorpe and Huggate.

Investigations by Herman Ramm in the 1960s suggested that the earliest phase of earthworks at one point along this route was represented by the holloway of an ancient track.

Before 1000 BC the mobile landscape was dotted with ceremonial monuments, meres, significant trees and other features, which would have been reached by a network of trackways. As the landscape became more ordered and enclosed, many of these trackways began to be used as boundaries. The tracks were already part of the way people organised the land and they would have made obvious boundaries as the landscape became more managed. These were the routes by which herds and travellers had passed across the land and they were part of both the mythical and practical understanding of the land. At the turn of the first millennium BC this landscape was enclosed and divided by long-distance boundaries that were laid out with respect to the features of the earlier landscape. This is an example of change that looks back to the traditional and the past but, at the same time, provides a revolutionary new way of ordering the land. Such measures are common throughout the 3000 years of our story. They show how important the past was to people's everyday view of the world but also that the way the landscape was understood and organised was always changing. This was not a timeless countryside of unending continuity but many features such as boundaries, barrows and tracks tended to survive for many centuries.

THREE

LANDSCAPES OF THE DEAD: CEMETERIES, PASTURES AND COMMUNITY, C.500 BC–AD 70

It is easy for archaeologists to focus entirely on the pots and flints they find, without considering how they related to peoples' lives. The changes in pottery styles, settlement types, burial rites and flint-working methods have helped to separate prehistory into different compartments. The Iron Age, Bronze Age and Neolithic (part of the broader Stone Age) were all devised as a way of ordering collections of artefacts. There is no doubt that techniques of working metal and stone did change throughout prehistory, but these technological advances were not the biggest influences on the changing lives of prehistoric populations.

This book is divided into period-based chapters for convenience only. Rather than be confined to specific periods, I have tried to take a broader view by looking at how the landscape and society changed over 3000 years. This period of change is not about distinctive 'ages' separate from one another, but about gradual and constant adaptation. One generation learned from its predecessor but also contributed its own unique addition to the cultural style of their community and also to the surrounding landscape. Sometimes these changes were radical, other times they were incidental. The changes were seldom imposed from outside but always took account of the past as it was perceived in the minds of the local people.

In this chapter we will deal with the landscapes of the Wolds during the middle and later centuries of the first millennium BC. This takes us from the early Iron Age to the first century AD, when the Roman forces marched northwards and crossed the Humber estuary into East Yorkshire, beginning 400 years of occupation.

East Yorkshire is famous for its Iron Age burials. Hundreds of these distinctive graves have been excavated and thousands more remain undisturbed below the ground. Elsewhere in the country, burials from this period are virtually unknown and for this reason East Yorkshire stands alone in Iron Age studies and society. Something different was going on here in the middle Iron Age between 500 and 100 BC. By contrast to other areas, the region also lacks the traditional Iron Age hill forts. These are found across most of the country and were large hilltop sites surrounded by huge enclosing ditches and banks. Some are known from the Wolds at the beginning of the first millennium BC, but there are none known after 800 BC.

In this chapter, we will try and imagine what the Wolds landscape was like in this period and trace the changes which took place in the lead-up to the Roman occupation of the region that began around AD 70. In doing so, we will be forced to question some of the assumptions that are often made about Iron Age East Yorkshire. The first is to do with where people were actually living and the second concerns the influence of the Roman presence on the landscape of settlements, field patterns and boundaries. By the end of the chapter it should be clear that the Wolds was not being used for settlement during the middle Iron Age, but instead, was probably a place for burial and pasture.

SQUARE BARROWS AND SETTLEMENT PATTERNS

The Iron Age burials were sometimes found alone, but were usually grouped into large cemeteries. A square ditch surrounded each grave and it is these that can be seen from the air as cropmarks (*23*). On aerial photographs, some of the large cemeteries look like frogspawn as the graves with surrounding ditches cluster together in large numbers. The deceased were sometimes given artefacts such as pottery or brooches and many were buried with joints of mutton or pork, carefully placed alongside the body. A small minority of graves contained rich metalwork such as swords, mirrors or items of jewellery. High-status objects were also found with the dismantled carts that were placed in some of the graves. The few people buried with carts reflected a special type of burial that was usually found outside the main cemeteries. The deceased in these cases may have been the wealthiest members of society but, equally, this kind of burial could have been given to people for other reasons. They may have committed acts of heroism or could even have been criminals or outcasts. We simply do not know.

There were very clear rules that governed the way people were laid to rest. Those buried with the remains of pigs were always oriented east to west, whilst

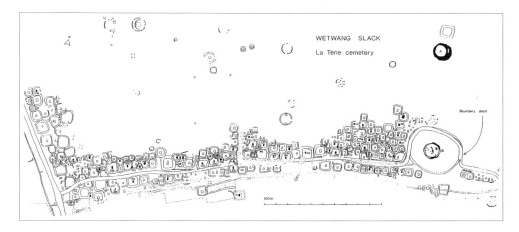

23 Excavation plan of square barrow cemetery at Wetwang Slack showing the linear ditch cutting through the barrows and then acting as boundary of the cemetery on its southern side. *From Dent* 1982

those with sheep were usually laid out north to south. The first group often had iron and bronze weaponry with them whilst the second group were often furnished with pots or brooches. There must have been a great deal of symbolic meaning given to the objects, animals and orientations but the specifics of these beliefs are not known to us.

The ditches surrounding the graves make them easy to see from the air. In one famous case near Burton Fleming these cropmarks can sometimes even be seen from the road verge at the side of the field, they are so clear. Due to the extensive coverage of the Wolds by aerial photographs we have a good idea of the distribution of cemeteries and burials. They are mainly found on the Wolds themselves, with far fewer burials in the surrounding lowlands. The majority of the cemeteries occur along the eastern side of the Wolds around Rudston and to the west of Driffield (*28*). This may reflect the easier access through the valleys on the eastern Wolds in contrast to the steep slopes of the western scarp.

What is not clear is where the people who buried their dead in these graves were living. The number of settlements from the period is very small, although there are more sites known from the last century of the first millennium BC after the burial rite had become abandoned. Archaeologists have assumed that the settlements contemporary with the burials are invisible archaeologically because ditches did not enclose them and because the buildings were made from posts that left little trace in the ground. It has generally been accepted that communities lived close by their cemeteries and therefore most people were living on the Wolds. This argument was fine until Iron Age settlements started to turn up from the low-lying areas to the east and west of the Wolds. The Vale of York produced a whole landscape full of Iron Age sites, showing that even though this area was wet in places, the Iron Age communities had used the raised sandy islands between creeks as sites for metalworking. To the east of the Wolds in the Hull Valley and plain of Holderness, further discoveries have been made of Iron Age settlements, some of them dating from the period of the burials. These discoveries have forced us to look more closely at the evidence from the Wolds and to ask whether people were actually living there alongside the cemeteries.

The first major cemetery to be excavated was at Arras on the high ground above Market Weighton (*11*). This is where the main road between Beverley and York crosses the Wolds and on a clear day it provides a breathtaking view over the Vale of York to the west. When I was at school I used to stand on the top of this hill by the roadside waiting for the bus, little realising that around me were the ploughed-down remains of hundreds of Iron Age graves. When they were excavated many of these graves were still visible on the ground as a series of low mounds, some of them with their square ditches still visible. The excavator, Canon Greenwell was a contemporary of J.R. Mortimer and he investigated a large number of burials here, including some with dismantled carts complete with bronze horse fittings as well as others with swords and other fine pieces of metalwork.

Many more burial sites were excavated in the 1980s and 1990s and most of these were on the eastern side of the Wolds around Driffield and Rudston. The most important findings were made along the bottom of one of the large dry valleys that leads out from the Wolds to the Hull Valley just to the west of Driffield. The excavations at Garton and Wetwang Slack took place because a huge gravel quarry threatened the archaeological remains (*23, 24* and *25*). Here, the traces of a total prehistoric landscape were preserved in the gravels at the bottom of the valley. This included barrows from the Neolithic and Bronze Age but also a massive Iron Age cemetery, as well as roundhouses and other traces of occupation from the same period. The fascinating findings from this site showed that the cemetery had co-existed alongside a settlement. As time went on both settlement and cemetery had been enclosed with ditches, until finally the cemetery fell out of use probably during the early part of the first century BC. Thereafter, the valley side itself was divided up with boundaries and settlement continued within a group of enclosures beyond the Roman Conquest and throughout the Roman occupation.

At first glance, the Wetwang/Garton discoveries confirmed what was already expected about Iron Age settlement. The large cemeteries had been placed alongside a contemporary settlement. According to this model, the population living in the roundhouses buried their dead close by, in a manner very familiar to

24 Iron Age roundhouses rescued from the gravel quarry at Wetwang-Garton Slack. *Courtesy Humber Archaeology Partnership*

those of us who grew up in a nucleated village complete with parish church and graveyard. However, the Wetwang Slack site is the only example of a settlement sitting alongside its cemetery despite numerous other cemeteries that have been excavated across the Wolds. Wetwang lies on low-lying ground on the valley floor on the way into the Wolds and only a few miles from the springs around Eastburn and Kirkburn (*9* and *11*). The presence of the settlement at Wetwang may be explained by its location close to the routes on the way into the heart of the Wolds from the Hull Valley and Holderness. In contrast, for the bulk of the chalk Wolds to the west and north, most of the cemeteries appear to lie on their own without adjacent settlements.

Since only a small number of Iron Age settlements have been found anywhere in East Yorkshire, it is difficult to be certain about where people lived and how the landscape was ordered. However, the infrequency of settlement sites may suggest that the Wolds was used largely for burial and not for permanent settlement. The majority of the population were probably living around the edges of the Wolds where a range of land and a constant supply of water from springs and streams were available. Recent archaeological work has begun to unearth these low-lying sites. Other communities would no doubt have been scattered throughout the lowland vales, making use of raised pieces of ground that were not subject to flooding and where good farming land was available. It is tempting to imagine that the dead of these communities were not buried close to home but were instead taken on their last journey onto the chalk Wolds

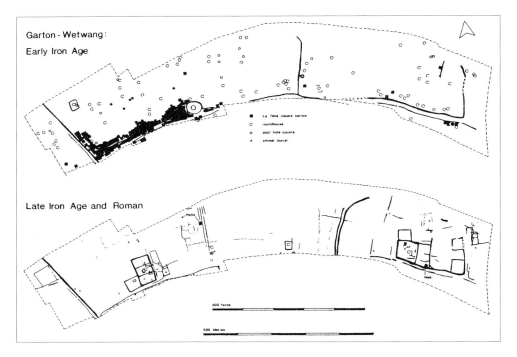

25 The changing landscape at Wetwang–Garton Slack during the late Iron Age and early Roman period. The lower plan shows the later phases of land division enclosing former open settlement and cemetery. *From Dent* 1983

and placed amongst the rest of the ancestors in cemeteries allocated to each community group or extended family. If we consider this possibility, the Wolds becomes a very different place in this period. It is not a landscape of settlement scattered with rural communities happily living off the land, but a landscape of the dead.

SHEEP FARMING ON THE CHALKLANDS

The well drained soils of the Wolds would have made ideal pasturage for sheep. The animals reared in the first millennium BC did not look like white fleecy clouds as most sheep do today, but would have been smaller, hardier and often with darker fleeces. Breeds like these still survive on the islands of St Kilda in the North Atlantic Ocean. Unlike cattle, sheep do not depend on a regular supply of water, nor do they need to be close to the home settlement all through the year. They are best herded in large numbers and allowed to roam and graze over wide expanses of land. The only way to find out about prehistoric livestock is through

26 Sheep gathering around the spring-fed mere at Burdale. This must have been one of the places where livestock and people came together during the times when the Wolds was used for grazing

recovering large collections of animal bone from excavated settlements of the period. These will tell us the range of animals that were reared by prehistoric communities but it is often difficult to ascertain the relative importance of one species against another. The bones of cattle are often over-represented which might simply be because they are larger in size and therefore preserve better, and not that they played a more important role in the economy. Equally the bones of animals kept close to the home settlement would be more likely to find their way into the pits and ditches under excavation.

The assemblages of bone from East Yorkshire Iron Age settlement sites contemporary with the burials tend to contain a large proportion of sheep. This is especially evident at Wetwang–Garton Slack, where sheep appear to have been the most important species. Other sites from the period also show a similar picture. It is tempting to imagine the expansive landscapes of the Wolds in the Iron Age being used mainly for sheep pasture. The land boundaries laid down in the later Bronze Age (1000–800 BC) would have provided a system of large, enclosed areas within which shepherds could have kept their flocks. These ditches and banks need not have been built as a barrier to the animals but more as a landscape marker, for the human communities to fix their boundaries. The presence of boundaries tells us that shepherds and flocks were not allowed simply to roam across this landscape but were confined within certain areas. We know that the later Bronze Age boundaries were still being used throughout the Iron Age as they were often respected by the burials and were used as part of the land division systems of the period surrounding the Roman Conquest. These pastures are likely to have been used by the same communities for several centuries and the knowledge of them would be passed down from one generation of shepherds to the next. In this way, the boundaries surrounding the pastures and the tracks leading to them would become associated with certain groups and given a kind of social identity.

Sheep farming is a seasonal affair. Large flocks of sheep cannot be left simply to roam around remote hillsides all year round. They must be watched carefully during lambing time and if necessary brought in for shelter and nurture. At other times of the year the flock must be brought together for shearing, but also for tupping and perhaps even dipping. Many of these tasks involve bringing the flocks down from the remote pastures into the home settlements. Today, it is only specialist farmers who possess flocks of sheep and one family or individual usually owns each flock. During the Iron Age, virtually all members of society would have been subsistence farmers and would probably have owned a number of sheep. The large flocks may well have belonged to a broad community of people. They may not have all lived in the same settlement but would have come together for seasonal gatherings and festivals. These could have taken place when the flocks were brought down from the pastures. Such events would have brought the communities together and would have cemented the relationship between the members of the group, but also between the community and their pastures up on the Wolds. The trackways leading from the wold-edge into the chalk downland would have been an important aspect of this, and well known to every member of the community.

At Wetwang one of the earliest features of the landscape excavated by John Dent and Tony Brewster was a trackway that ran along the bottom of the valley (27). It provided the focus for burial monuments from the Neolithic and Bronze Age but was also respected by the layout of the Iron Age cemetery (23 and 25). This track, which led from the headwater springs of the Hull Valley into the heart of the Wolds, had been in use for many centuries. A whole series of tracks would have led from the lowlands of Holderness into the Wolds from the east. Some would have taken the higher ground, following ridges, whilst others seem to have run along the bottom of the broad valleys. These valleys become narrower and steeper as they penetrate the chalkland. A distribution map of the cemeteries and burials shows that many are concentrated along these routeways

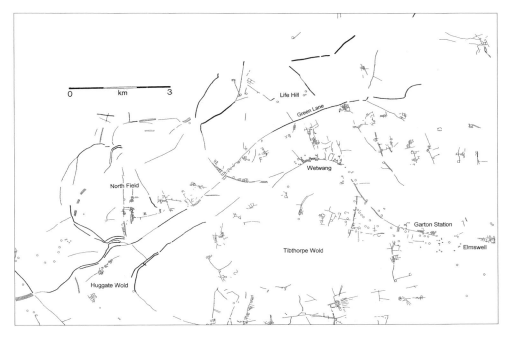

27 Cropmarks between Huggate and Elmswell. The Sledmere Green Lane earthwork survived into the late Iron Age and was used as a major boundary in this period. The pattern of ditches on the slopes above Wetwang was clearly based on this earthwork. There were very few ditches or enclosures north of the Green Lane. The valley floor trackway curves up from Garton Station to Wetwang. *After Stoertz 1997*

both along the valley floors and on top of the ridges (*28*). The cemeteries would have become places of community identity where the collective dead were laid to rest. Places like this which symbolised the group would have been important, especially if the group members did not live in one single settlement but were spread about the lowland plains in discrete hamlets. The shepherds would have passed by these burial places on a regular basis and each time would have been reminded of the recently deceased. Some would have been dear to them whilst for others they would recall the funeral festivities but not the living person. For the rest of the community, visits to the cemeteries may only have been made at those times of the year when the sheep were brought together or at funerals.

The cemeteries belonged to the community and so too did the pastures and the flocks. If the same groups owned both sheep and cemeteries, then the burials could well have served as landscape markers, linking the living group with the pasture and the tracks that led there. The high concentration of burials along these tracks would suggest that a number of communities used the same track, leading to different pasture areas. The burials, with their distinctive square ditch surrounding the grave, were placed in the landscape with great care. In some cases they were sited next to the side ditch of a trackway that can still be seen as a cropmark on an aerial photograph (*23*). In other places, they were located close to round barrows that were already old and had first been erected over 1000 years earlier.

This interpretation of Iron Age landscape and community is based on what little evidence we have available. I have made links between the cemeteries and large-scale sheep farming and suggest that the Wolds was a place of burial and pasture with most people actually living on the lower ground surrounding the chalk. This model is by no means accepted by everyone working in the area and may be challenged by future discoveries. However, to my mind it provides a very pleasing holistic explanation for the cemeteries and their links with settlement and farming and opens windows on the whole elusive idea of the sense of community that was enjoyed by Iron Age people in this area.

LAND DIVISION AND SETTLEMENT EXPANSION DURING THE LATER IRON AGE

The changes to the archaeology and landscape that occur at the end of the Iron Age also require explanation and this can be found in the breakdown of the system. The idea of a region made up of tracts of landscape that served different purposes and had different identities or characters is something that was familiar in the Middle Ages but is not so prevalent today. During the Iron Age, the Wolds may have been a landscape of the dead and would have been seen by the communities living around it as a special place, with unique and often mysterious qualities. This is an idea that emerges again and again throughout the late prehistoric, Roman and medieval periods and we will come back to it later. Based on his work in the Foulness Valley to the west of the Wolds, Peter Halkon has suggested that there might have been a different type of landscape in the Iron Age and Roman periods. He suggested that it was an area devoted to industrial activities such as metalworking and pottery production and complemented zones of settlement and farming in other areas.

Towards the end of the first millennium BC, during the late Iron Age, the archaeology changes. The number of burials and barrows started to dwindle, until, by the first century AD, the tradition had died out. At the same time, the landscape started to be divided up again and enclosed with boundary ditches. This time they were very different to those constructed 800 years earlier during the later Bronze Age. Instead of long-distance linear earthworks dividing whole tracts of countryside, the late Iron Age ditches enclosed land into large rectangular or square enclosures. These were sometimes found alongside trackways as rows of adjacent enclosures and for this reason have been called 'ladder settlements'. In

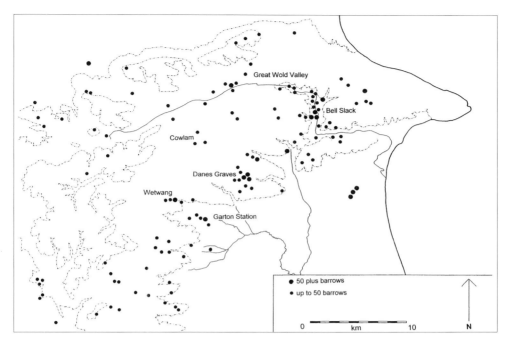

28 Iron Age cemeteries in the northern Wolds. Most barrow groups are known only from aerial photography. They concentrate in the valleys that give access to the Wolds from the Hull Valley and Holderness. *After Stead 1979 and Stoertz 1997*

some cases, they do indeed contain roundhouses and would therefore have been occupation sites but in others, there is no trace of domestic occupation. Similar enclosed sites occur in many parts of the north in the centuries leading up to the Roman Conquest. In East Yorkshire, they continue to be used and developed after the Roman Conquest and many survive through into the second or early third century AD.

At Wetwang Slack these developments have been clearly revealed. The main cemetery fell out of use during the early first century BC when the area was enclosed by ditched boundaries (*25* and *27*). The formerly open settlement was hereafter confined within enclosure ditches and a large square enclosure was laid out on the south facing slopes of the valley side. This enclosure was aligned upon the already ancient banks and ditches of the Green Lane earthwork, described in chapter two that had been constructed as a land boundary back at the beginning of the first millennium BC. All across the Wolds, a similar picture has been revealed as the landscape was divided and enclosed at the same time as the cemeteries started to fall out of use. It seems reasonable to assume that the two phenomena were linked.

29 Looking for clues in the earth

These changes did not take place suddenly but were probably spread over a century or two. For the communities involved, they must have taken place over a number of generations and may have been the subject of some tension. We could perhaps imagine a traditional element within the society who felt it was sacrilege not to carry on with the old ways of burial. Older members of the community may have been offended by the views of the younger generation and affronted by the way they showed no respect for their ancestors and the history of their community. At the same time, the division and enclosure of land could also have been a contentious issue as families began to claim land for themselves that had previously been the property of the whole community. We can only imagine how people felt about these changes to the landscape and we do not know what social or economic forces were in play.

However, it is clear that the old social landscape of sheep farming and burial on the Wolds must have broken down. Much of the land that had previously been used for large-scale sheep pasturage began to be enclosed and occupied as smaller groups took communal land for themselves. This may of course have involved people moving from the settled lowlands to the Wolds and taking land for settlement and farming that had previously been used purely for burial and pasture. The community was gradually losing its land and along with that must

30 A single square barrow under excavation at Melton, near Brough

have gone the whole practice of sheep farming on a large scale. The cemeteries too were falling out of use. As fewer and fewer burials were made in them, they must have lost their meaning as symbols of community identity. This function for the cemeteries was becoming less and less important as the whole sheep farming landscape was also breaking down. The simultaneous disintegration of previous burial practices and land division underlines how interdependent these aspects of society must have been.

This period of land division and settlement expansion was the first of three similar episodes of intensification to hit the Wolds over the next 2000 years. Together, these developments form part of a long-term sequence of cycles in the landscape. These cycles keep on turning right up to the present day. The late Iron Age settlements became the rural settlements of Roman East Yorkshire occupied by the British subjects of the Roman Empire. However, these people were not foreigners. They were the direct descendants of the communities who had lived here during the later Iron Age. The Roman Conquest may have brought with it a change in political control and paved the way for a ready supply of mass-produced pottery and some coinage, but it did not appreciably alter the way that the landscape of the Wolds was organised or occupied. These changes had already started to take place 150 years earlier.

FOUR

FROM ROUNDHOUSES TO VILLAS: ROMANISED AGRICULTURAL LANDSCAPES, FIRST—FIFTH CENTURIES AD

One of my first archaeology jobs was in south-west Wales. A lost Roman road running from Carmarthen towards the west coast had been rediscovered from aerial photographs. We were given the opportunity of following it up on the ground and dug a trench through the road's causeway. The local paper became interested, so I spent some time telling the young reporter all about archaeology, Roman roads and the ins and outs of the Roman occupation in Britain. When I saw the article, I realised that he had told a very different story. The headline read 'Troublesome Britons delay road scheme' and the article began something like this:

> Nero banged his fist on the marble table. He was not having a good day. The engineers who were building the road out of Maridunum had run into opposition from the locals again.

This anecdote highlights some of the difficulties of understanding the real history of the Roman period in Britain. There are so many stereotypes and assumptions that have to be overturned before you start. Roman archaeology used to be led by the historical record and the political history of emperors and military campaigns. This approach had seen the Roman Empire as a civilising force bringing barbaric indigenous populations forward and introducing them to a market economy, written language and regular baths. Over the last twenty years, the focus has shifted so that we now acknowledge that the indigenous societies encountered by the Romans were already highly organised and complex. The culture and society of each Roman province was unique and each displayed a mixture of indigenous and Roman lifestyles. Romanisation was a two-way process and the imperialists in Rome learnt as much from the subjugated peoples as the other way round.

Another misconception was that the existing society and landscape were transformed as soon as the Roman legions arrived. In many parts of the country, especially the north, the Roman occupation was a political takeover that had little effect on the everyday lives of most people. They continued to live in the same settlements and lived the same lifestyles as before. Change did occur but it took time and in some areas like East Yorkshire the landscape of settlements, boundaries and farming practice did not drastically alter for at least 100 years.

There had been great changes to the Wolds landscape in the centuries leading up to the Roman Conquest of AD 43. Much of the old pastoral landscape of large-scale sheep farming had been enclosed and inhabited. The traditional burial rites were dying out and social and economic life now revolved around the household rather than large dispersed communities. This process continued after the Conquest but was not obviously affected by the Roman presence at least for another 100 years.

There are many archaeological sites known from this period and the number is still growing. Excavations consistently show that the rural landscape outside of the main towns was not drastically affected by the Roman presence until at least AD 200. The number of Romanised mass produced pottery sherds that turn up on these sites is small and the locally produced handmade pottery styles continued to be used right up to the third century. During the third century this landscape did change. Settlement sites were abandoned and several highly Romanised villas were constructed usually close to the towns. They reflect an increasingly Romanised way of life for certain members of society. The management of the rural farming economy may well have become more intensive and was probably run from these estate centres.

THE ARRIVAL OF THE ROMANS IN EAST YORKSHIRE

The Roman legions arrived on the Kent coast in AD 43 and quickly established political control of southern England. The societies here had been in contact with the Roman world through trade and alliances and many of their leaders were ready to adopt a new Romanised lifestyle. At first, the Humber Estuary was used as the northern frontier of the province and for nearly 30 years the people on the north bank traded with the Roman Empire on the other side of the river. At Redcliff, on the banks of the Humber near Ferriby, a trading settlement has been excavated with many imported finewares, coins and other exotic items from the Romanised lands to the south. We do not know where these imported goods were going. In the entire north of England, only one high-status political centre has been found from this period and that was at Stanwick in North Yorkshire. In the south, this period of contact before the Roman Conquest saw the emergence of a group of high-status political and economic centres known as *oppida*. They are assumed to have been the centres of power for tribal groups in contact with the Romans. We do not know if such places existed in East Yorkshire, as none have yet been located.

The Roman legions crossed the Humber around AD 70 and seem to have met with little resistance. For East Yorkshire, there is none of the colourful prose associated with Vespasian's march through Dorset and Hampshire, laying siege to British strongholds and hill forts. We know from historical sources that the Romans knew the people of East Yorkshire as *Parisi*. This was the name given to the local inhabitants at the time of the Conquest and it was also the name used for the administrative territory or *civitas* based in East Yorkshire throughout the Roman occupation. We do not know how meaningful the term was to the indigenous people or whether there were smaller tribal groups within the region. The *Brigantes* were a much larger grouping and occupied the rest of Yorkshire to the north and west. They were probably a confederation of smaller dispersed tribal groups who came together to resist the growing Roman threat in the south. If we are to believe the classical histories, then the *Brigantes* were less friendly towards the Romans than the *Parisi*. The decision to march into Yorkshire and the north may well have been taken to quell this resistance as the system of alliances with these people had broken down.

The Romans established a new road from the fort at Brough-on-Humber along the western side of the Wolds to York, where a massive legionary fortress was set up. Other forts were established at Hayton, Malton and probably Stamford Bridge in the early years of the Conquest (*31*). Only Malton continued to be used as a military garrison after the first century. Elsewhere in East Yorkshire, the military presence was scaled down, with York remaining as a major military base for the duration of the occupation. The political and civil sides of Roman rule soon replaced military garrisons and this suggests that the occupation of East Yorkshire was largely peaceful. In much of Southern Britain, a political culture in the Roman mould was established whereby the existing local rulers were encouraged to act as the new regional officials. In the north and west, where military garrisons were needed throughout the occupation, the Romanisation of the indigenous elites cannot have been as effective.

The Roman towns were the first urban centres in East Yorkshire. No prehistoric settlements had been as densely populated or economically diverse.

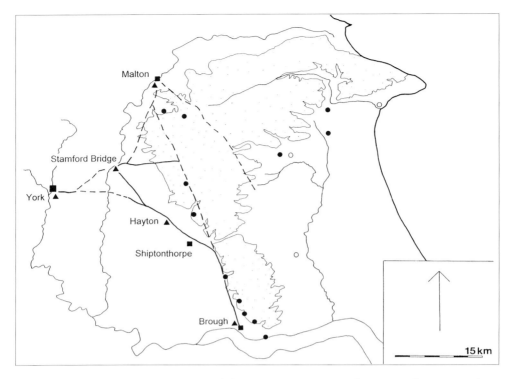

31 Major Romano-British sites in East Yorkshire. Towns are represented as squares, forts as triangles and villas or other important rural sites as circles. The open circles represent the modern towns of Bridlington, Driffield and Beverley where some Romano-British evidence has come to light

They were not on the scale of York or many of the larger towns further south, but for the region they represented a huge cultural change. We know about them partly through archaeology and partly through the documentary sources. There are Roman itineraries that list the main towns of the province of Britannia, as well as the distances between them in Roman miles. For East Yorkshire, whose administrative name was the *Civitas Parisiorum*, there are four places listed: *Derventio, Delgovitia, Petuaria* and *Praetorio*. We know from an inscription found during excavations at Brough that here was the town of *Petuaria*, the administrative capital of the *civitas*. This was close to where the legions must have first landed and its situation commanded the Humber crossing point. The town developed slowly following the establishment of a fort. By the second century, *Petuaria* appears to have had its own theatre. Excavations have shown how a sizeable civilian settlement grew up on the site with occupation extending beyond the defences of the town. It must have been a centre for trade and commerce and the place where the trappings of Roman culture would have been most visible.

A number of villas are known from the hinterland of the town, although most of these were not established until 200 years after the Conquest.

Derventio was obviously derived from the River Derwent and is usually associated with the fort and town at Malton. A wealthy civilian settlement grew up outside the fort and thrived as a market and economic centre throughout the Roman occupation. Like Brough, Malton was surrounded by a series of Romanised settlements, whose occupants had adopted many Roman building techniques and other aspects of material culture. Both towns acted as cultural centres, which introduced Roman lifestyles to the local populations. However, this process was very slow. It was not until the third century that the indigenous inhabitants began to use mass-produced pottery and to build Roman style houses with stone foundations and rectangular plans.

Delgovitia has not yet been located on the ground. The antiquarians of the eighteenth and nineteenth centuries thought it might have been at Millington or even Wetwang but more recent opinion has placed it either at Malton (moving *Derventio* to Stamford Bridge) or the recently discovered small town at Shiptonthorpe, just north of Market Weighton. The fourth name on the list, *Praetorio*, may be another name for *Petuaria* or alternatively could have been used for York or even an otherwise unrecorded town on the east coast near Bridlington. There was probably a Roman road that went in this direction across the Wolds, but as yet there has been no definitive archaeological evidence for a Roman urban centre here. Bearing in mind that this coastline has been eroding away into the sea for centuries, this is perhaps not surprising as the remains of the town could have been lost to coastal erosion. Despite this, there have been recent discoveries of Roman occupation along this coastline to add to what was already known of the late Roman signal station at Filey.

RURAL SETTLEMENT IN THE EARLY ROMAN PERIOD

Two sites were excavated in 2000 on the western edge of Bridlington, away from the sea. They were within 500m of each other and both showed evidence for late Iron Age and Roman period settlement. Sewerby Cottage Farm is now a housing estate, but before the houses were built archaeological excavations took place. The work by *On-Site Archaeology* revealed part of a settlement or farmstead that began around 100 BC when a square barrow was constructed alongside a linear boundary ditch. There was some scattered occupation before the Roman Conquest but then the site became part of an extensive agricultural complex during the first and second centuries AD. Its inhabitants were farmers, practising both arable cultivation and livestock rearing. Three kilns were probably used to process the harvested crops and in the north of the site a system of droveways and ditches would have channelled the movement of animals during shearing, dipping or perhaps milking. The animal bones did not survive well and it was not possible to determine whether the farm was reliant on sheep, cattle or both. The farm was abandoned during the early third century AD and the latest pottery was dated to around AD 250.

The nearby excavations at Bempton Lane were carried out by *West Yorkshire Archaeology Service*, and they found a late Iron Age settlement dated to before the Roman occupation. This site continued to flourish throughout the second and third centuries AD. It may be that following the demise of a neighbouring settlement at Cottage Farm in the third century, the Bempton Lane site took over the management of a larger estate, which included the lands of their neighbours. It is hard to say whether these two rural farmsteads lay on the outskirts of an early Roman town at Bridlington or not. From experience elsewhere in the region, we would not be able to tell this from the kinds of pottery styles and building types found within rural settlements on the margins of a town. At most of the rural settlements close to the town of Brough, there is very little Romanised pottery and few Roman-style buildings until the third century.

We have already mentioned the excavations at Wetwang Slack. During the late Iron Age, this settlement site was enclosed by ditches that were part of a much more extensive system of land division. The ditches that divided up the land here tended to hang off the ancient earthwork that ran along the ridge followed by the Sledmere Green Lane (*25* and *27*). As time went on, this landscape became more and more intensively occupied with further settlements springing up within their own enclosures. These were not isolated sites but were all linked by the network of ditches that divided the lands of each settlement from its neighbour. The process of change at Wetwang had begun during the second or first century BC when the cemetery was slowly abandoned and the new ditches dug. The Roman Conquest had little direct effect and the same communities must have continued to live and farm this area for centuries after the first century BC.

The same sequence is known all over the Wolds and throughout East Yorkshire. Many Roman period settlements have origins before the Conquest and this suggests that the Roman presence did little to change the way that people lived or where they resided. The distinctive sites such as Wetwang, known as 'ladder settlements' tend to begin during the late Iron Age but continue to be occupied throughout the early Roman period. One or two examples, such as Wheldrake, have no obvious Iron Age origin but these are the exceptions to the rule. The ladder sites are best seen on aerial photographs and there are many examples scattered across the Wolds (*32* and *colour plate 28*). They consist of a series of rectangular or square ditched enclosures arranged along the side of a

32 Aerial photograph of Blealands Nook enclosures. These ditches were excavated by Mortimer and were laid out in the early Roman period. The Sledmere Green Lane is followed by the track running from the top to bottom of the shot. *Courtesy English Heritage crown copyright*

ditched trackway or boundary. As time went on, more and more enclosures were added to the string and some of these sites are over 1km long. There is no doubt that some were used as settlements, as roundhouses have been found inside the enclosures. Others may simply have served as paddocks for animals.

At present, the ladder sites tell us two things; one to do with dating, the other concerned with their distribution on the Wolds and surrounding lowlands. Firstly, the landscape changes that took place at the end of the Iron Age continued until the late second or early third century when most of these sites were abandoned. As we have already seen, this coincides with the rise in villas and may indicate a change in the management of the farming economy. Those ladder sites that do continue beyond the third century were often altered at this time and new enclosures were added. Secondly, the ladder settlements are mainly found on the Wolds although there are some examples from the surrounding lowlands. This point is crucial to our long-term story as it indicates that the distinction between the Wolds and the vales may have remained in place even when the chalklands were being farmed and occupied. We must be cautious making this latter point, as ditched sites such as these ladder settlements tend to show up much more easily on the light calcareous soils of the chalk than on the clays that surround it. The

Humber wetlands project has recently identified Roman period enclosures on the lowlands but these are by no means as numerous as they are on the Wolds.

The early Roman sequence is well represented around the town of Brough on the north bank of the Humber estuary (*31*). Anyone driving to Hull from the west along the M62 cannot fail to appreciate the topographic setting of this corridor. As you pass by Goole, the Wolds can be seen off in the distance as a low ridge on the horizon, stretching off to the north. At Melton, the Wolds scarp towers over the road on its northern side, leaving little space for flatter ground before the estuary itself. This is where the Wolds Way begins. Here, the strip of land along the base of the scarp slope, on the edge of the Wolds, was densely occupied during the later Iron Age and Roman period. There are many sites, such as North Cave, Elloughton and Brantingham where occupation began during the Iron Age and continued beyond the Conquest. Before the Conquest, the inhabitants of these places would have been highly aware of the Roman presence on the other side of the Humber. The trading site at Redcliff was only miles away and some of its exotic products found their way onto these indigenous settlements.

At Melton, there is a ladder settlement that runs parallel to the existing road at the foot of the Wolds scarp. Along with many other people, I was involved with the excavation of this site during the summer and winter of 2004-5 (*colour plates 28* and *29*). The Highways Agency had planned to redesign the junction, which involved building slip roads and roundabouts on both sides of the existing road. The ladder site with its enclosures and central ditched trackway was known from aerial photography and much of it had to be excavated before the road construction could begin. The writing up and analysis of the site findings is not yet complete but we know the basic sequence. The landscape was first divided up by huge north–south linear earthworks that were sited deliberately on a Bronze Age round barrow. These ditches are featured in *colour plate 29* and in *colour plate 28* and can be seen in the south-western corner of the latter picture. The barrow was an unexpected find and sat just on the northern edge of the A63 dual carriageway. The boundary ditches were probably dug during the middle Iron Age and were contemporary with a north–south trackway, 100m to the east, which must have provided access between the high ground of the Wolds and the banks of the estuary to the south. The enclosures of the ladder site grew up around an east–west trackway which was probably first used during the Iron Age. It was not provided with side ditches until the later centuries of the Iron Age but before the Roman Conquest. As with Wetwang, the landscape here became more and more divided and enclosed from the later Iron Age onwards. The earliest occupation was a small Iron Age settlement of roundhouses, paddocks and a midden dump on one side of the east–west track.

This site did not continue for long after the Conquest when the inhabitants probably moved a short distance along the track to the west. During the early centuries of the Roman occupation, the landscape we excavated formed part of the fields and boundaries belonging to this settlement. The dead were often buried alongside the boundaries and at the junction of the two trackways. At the start of the third century, pottery runs out, suggesting that the site was abandoned at this time. The reasons for this change are not immediately clear but there may be a clue from some older excavations only kilometres away on the top of the Wolds scarp at Welton Wold. There was a large Roman villa, which was the earliest example in the region, beginning during the second century. As with the other villas, the settlement grew in size and wealth reaching a peak during the third and fourth centuries when the site was re-organised.

AGRICULTURAL INTENSIFICATION IN THE THIRD CENTURY

The indigenous settlements tended to die out during the early third century at the same time as the villas sprang up. What we might be seeing here are drastic changes to landownership and estate management. During the late second and early third century AD, the Wolds landscape was taken in by new landlords who eventually controlled large areas, setting up estate centres and furnishing them with lavish Romanised architecture. There are many examples of landscape change in the third century. Not only do many of the indigenous style settlements fall out of use but also there were new settlement complexes using Roman building styles and pottery.

During the third century a number of pottery production centres emerged, which then supplied the villas with their fine tableware and cooking vessels. The villas at Rudston and Langton developed at this time but both replaced earlier indigenous style farmsteads (*11*). Villa settlements like these were often provided with large rectangular stone-founded buildings, mosaic floors, bathhouses and murals. They were not only the residences of wealthy and powerful families but also the centres of large agricultural estates. At Wharram Percy, the boundaries of the Roman settlement were modified in the third century and two successive crop-drying kilns were constructed.

There are many crop driers found in association with the villas on the Wolds and this has led to suggestions that the changes of the third century were related to an increase in arable cultivation. At Welton villa, the third- and fourth-century phases had fourteen crop driers suggesting the management of the harvest on an industrial scale. Recent excavations at Cat Babbleton show

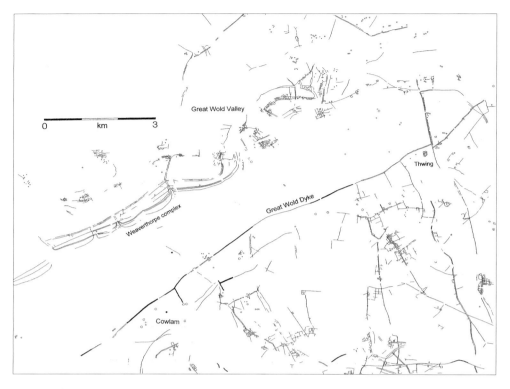

33 Cropmarks around the Great Wold valley. The empty space defined by the Great Wold Dyke and the multiple ditches at Weaverthorpe is clearly shown. This area must have been a longstanding pasture zone and was respected even by the encroaching settlement and cultivation of the Roman period. *After Stoertz 1997*

that some major land boundaries were constructed during the third and fourth centuries and at Swaythorpe there was also re-organisation in this period. Both sites lie on the high Wolds and many of the other linear earthworks known from this area may also have been dug in the Roman period.

THE SURVIVAL OF PASTURES

There were some areas of the Wolds that do not appear to have been occupied or divided with ditches. The aerial photographic plots show certain places usually on the higher ground where very few ditches, enclosures or any signs of habitation are visible. In some cases, these areas were actually enclosed by ditches that had been in use as land boundaries since the Iron Age at least. The most impressive example lies along the south side of the Great Wold Valley where the aerial photographic plots show a large area totally devoid of cropmarks of any kind (*33*). This rectangular zone is limited by the long distance boundary of the Great Wold Dyke on the south and by an impressive system of ditched droveways on the north. These appear to have been constructed during the Iron Age and would have funnelled the movement of livestock from the open pasture down to the settled lands along the valley floor. It seems likely that this area remained as a dedicated pasture throughout the Roman period as it was precisely the zone used as pasture during the Middle Ages when the townships were arranged along the valley and their settlements strung out along the Gypsey Race. There may be other areas on the Wolds that were not divided and enclosed by ditches during the Roman period. Another blank space is visible in the distribution of cropmark sites to the north of Tibthorpe (*27*). This area was known as Tibthorpe Wold in the post-medieval period and was probably used as pasture throughout the Middle Ages (*43*). Like the southern slopes of the Great Wold Valley, it may have been respected and used for pasture consistently since the Iron Age.

LATER ROMANO-BRITISH LANDSCAPES

There is no doubt that the Wolds landscape was reorganised again during the third century AD. The changes appear to be related to the management of agricultural production and involved the setting up of rural estates to centralise the farming of large areas. The third-century transformations in landscape and agricultural economy may have been more apparent on the Wolds than the surrounding vales. Was this to do with the topography and agricultural potential of the chalkland or was it rooted in the distinctive rights of landholding that prevailed here? The tide of intensive management and farming that flowed over the Wolds in the third century was the culmination of the expansion, which began at the end of the Iron Age.

There were more people living and farming on the Wolds during the Roman period than during the Iron Age. Similarly, there were fewer people living here after the fifth century when Roman political control was ended. Colin Hayfield's fieldwalking survey of Wharram Percy parish has shown that the Roman period settlement pattern in Wharram parish was far denser than the Iron Age or Anglo-Saxon equivalents.

The end of the Roman occupation of Britain is still shrouded in mystery. We know that there was increasing unrest throughout the empire during the fourth and fifth centuries and there is historical evidence that tribes from outside the empire were beginning to threaten the imperial frontiers. The signal stations of the east coast including one at Filey were a response to the growing military threat. There was also economic unrest as the political grip of Rome was loosened and greater autonomy felt by individual provinces and their leaders. There may have been a taxation crisis at this time where increasingly powerful landlords stopped paying their taxes and deliberately distanced themselves from the empire and its administrative structure.

At a local level, the archaeological evidence can sometimes be difficult to interpret. At the villa sites the material evidence, comprising coinage and pottery supplies, simply ran out by the early fifth century, coinciding with the time when Rome stopped governing the province of Britannia. The big question is whether these settlements continued to be occupied or whether they were abandoned. We cannot identify or date occupation after the early fifth century because there were no durable datable artefacts.

At a small number of rural settlements in East Yorkshire, there is evidence for continuity of some kind. For instance, excavations at Elmswell identified late Roman and early Anglo-Saxon material on the same site. Likewise, the town of Malton had very late Roman occupation and has also produced evidence from the Anglo-Saxon and later periods. At Sherburn in the Vale of Pickering, a late Roman settlement was abandoned probably because of flooding. The inhabitants may then have moved to drier ground to establish the large settlement at West Heslerton that thrived between the sixth and eighth centuries AD. At Wharram Percy, the inhabitants of the Roman period farm may have continued to occupy the site as there is evidence for their presence from the Anglo-Saxon period.

The system of villa estates and towns of the third and fourth centuries appears to have broken down at the beginning of the fifth. There follows a period of several centuries when we simply do not know where people lived or how the landscape was inhabited. By the seventh and eighth centuries, the Wolds looked very different to the intensively farmed and managed agricultural landscapes of the Roman period. Despite these changes, it appears that many boundaries and trackways survived the social upheaval.

FIVE

SETTLEMENT PATTERNS AND RURAL ESTATES ON THE POST-ROMAN WOLDS

APPROACHES TO EARLY MEDIEVAL STUDIES

The time period covered by this chapter runs from the fifth century to the eleventh century. Historically, the period is sandwiched between the end of the Roman occupation and the Norman Conquest of 1066. There are many different ways to tell the story of this era. For some, it provides the foundations for the English nation, the beginning of the English language and a starting point for the ancestral line of the kings and queens who populated traditional school history books. The political history tells that a dominant Anglo-Saxon political control spread from the east. From the middle of the ninth century there was an influx of people and power from the Scandinavian countries, bringing the Danish and Norwegian languages and giving rise to the myths of Viking rape and pillage.

Traditionally, the history of this period has been seen through a Christian perspective, influenced by the writings of Bede in the early eighth century. According to this viewpoint these centuries saw an endless struggle between pagans and Christians. To the historian, the period provides some of the earliest source material. There are many surviving annals, land charters, legends, stories and histories written before the Norman Conquest, but very few for East Yorkshire. For archaeologists, the period is distinct from the preceding Roman centuries. The archaeological remains of settlements and cemeteries show that the cultural influences were coming from across the North Sea but that a great deal of indigenous Romano-British influence remained. The ideas of massive folk migrations and the replacement of the Romano-British population no longer stand. It is now accepted that the vast majority of people using Anglo-Saxon pots and burial rites and even those speaking the Old English language could trace their ancestry back to Romano-British stock.

Links between periods are often difficult to detect because the nature and quality of the evidence is often very different from one period to another. For instance, the large quantities of Roman pottery found on sites between the second and fourth centuries are absent from occupation sites dating from after the fifth century. This does not necessarily mean that these sites had become abandoned and the populations fled but that the social and economic structures they inhabited had changed. Despite the obvious changes that took place in terms of language, political organisation and cultural and social life, we should remember that the same families are likely to have inhabited the same fields and pastures. This is the story of a changing landscape, but of one whose past was never forgotten. The same viewpoints, valleys and trackways known to the people of the Wolds in 200 would also have been familiar to their descendants in 700. We sometimes forget these connections across long periods of time when we divide history into neat compartments.

34 A longstanding trackway, now a well-used footpath. Shortlands Dale on the western Wolds

THE WOLDS

It was common amongst the topographers and travellers of the early modern period to refer to the area as the Wolds, or Yorkshire Wolds. In the 1750s the landscape of the chalkland was very different to that of the surrounding vales. The fields had not been enclosed nor the land improved. Meanwhile, the lowlands of Holderness and the vales were being drained, hedged and farmed with new technologies and with a fervour that sometimes amounted to missionary zeal. We know that by the seventeenth century the place was known as the Wolds but how far back in time does this name go and had it always used for the same area and in the same way?

The earliest references to the Wolds do not refer to the whole district but to small portions of it. These are often called *wold* or *wald* and appear in land charters and grants from as early as the tenth century. A charter for Newbald dating from 963 talks about the boundary heading 'from the street east right up on a wold'. In the period after the Norman Conquest pieces of land continue to be be referred to as *wold*. There is an example from 1180 that uses the word *waldum* to refer to the area later known as East Heslerton Wold. Another example comes from Huggate where Huggate Wold was also known as *wald*.

After the thirteenth century, these references to specific parts of the Wolds are usually given a township name. By this time, each township had succeeded in appropriating some wold land for itself and these names, such as Middleton Wold and Goodmanham Wold, have stuck to this day. Despite this, it seems likely that the Wolds was recognised as a district before its land was divided amongst the townships. In 1208, the village of Garton was described as lying *in waldo* and in 1301, Bainton was referred to as being located in *super waldas*. From the thirteenth century onwards, there are many references to villages lying 'on the Wolds' and some villages, such as Garton-on-the-Wolds and Middleton-on-the-Wolds still retain this phrase in their names today.

The name Wolds comes from the Old English word *wald* and there are several other areas in England, which also get their names from this root. There are Wolds in Nottinghamshire and Leicestershire and the Weald in Kent which all take their names from the Old English *wald*. The word itself must originate from before the Norman Conquest and is thought to be as early as the eighth century. Before the eleventh century, it is believed to have referred to woodland but after that the name was used to describe high, open waste ground. The meaning of *wald* appears to have changed around the time of the Norman Conquest. The amount of woodland on the Wolds was very small at the time of Domesday Book (1086) and was probably restricted to isolated patches with more extensive tracts in the Beverley area. The Yorkshire Wolds is unlikely to have been named after its woodland

35 Looking east from Holme on Spalding Moor towards the distant scarp slope of the Wolds

and the meaning of open landscape, current after the eleventh century is more fitting.

Harold Fox has suggested that the Wolds in other parts of the country were characterised by wood pasture during the seventh and eighth centuries. He has hinted that the Yorkshire Wolds may have looked wooded because of the woodland that lined the scarp slopes on its northern and western edges. However, the historian, Chris Wickham, has suggested that the word *wald* may not have been used to describe the appearance of the landscape but instead referred to the rights held over the land in the centuries following the Roman occupation. If this is true, then the Wolds may have been wooded, open or a mixture of both, for it was the nature of landholding that set them apart, not their vegetation or land-use.

This idea would fit well if the post Roman landscape of the Yorkshire Wolds was generally open and pastoral. There may have been isolated stands of woodland but it is unlikely to have contained extensive or continuous wooded areas. The area certainly appears to have been occupied in a very different way to the surrounding lowlands between the fifth and ninth centuries. The settlements and cemeteries of the post Roman population tended to cluster around the edges of the Wolds while the interior of the chalkland was largely uninhabited. We will see in this chapter and the next how this landscape was marginal to the main centres of settlement and was used mainly for pasture, in very much the same way as the middle Iron Age landscape described in chapter three. In this sense, the Yorkshire Wolds enjoyed a very similar post Roman history to the Wolds of Nottinghamshire and Leicestershire. However, the idea that the Wolds was largely uninhabited pasture between the fifth and ninth centuries is not generally accepted and the evidence for this needs to be carefully presented.

ANGLO-SAXON SETTLEMENT

Before we can understand the landscape of the Wolds in the post Roman centuries it is important to think about where people were living throughout East Yorkshire at this time. Where were the main centres of population? Were settlements scattered evenly across the region or were they concentrated in certain favoured areas? How different was the Anglo-Saxon settlement pattern from the Roman period? These are straightforward questions but they do not have easy answers because the nature of the evidence is patchy. From archaeology, we have a large number of cemeteries and more isolated burials from this period. As we have already seen for the Iron Age, the pattern of burials should not be taken to reflect the distribution of settlements, as communities did not always bury their dead close to where they were living.

On the northern edge of the Wolds, just below the steep escarpment, lies the site of West Heslerton where wind-blown sands have buried and preserved the remains of a large and long-lived Anglo-Saxon settlement. The site is part of an extensive multi-period landscape with traces of Neolithic, Bronze Age, Iron Age and Roman period occupation. The Anglo-Saxon site contained evidence for many post-built halls as well as a large inhumation cemetery, located close to the settlement (*11*). This site is nationally important and has given us a valuable insight into the lives of an Anglo-Saxon community between the fifth and seventh centuries. It cannot by itself tell us about the wider settlement pattern or indeed how the Wolds was being occupied and used at this time. However, its situation is important as it lies on the wold-edge in a position ideally suited to exploit the varied resources of the high Wolds to the south as well as the low lying wetter lands to the north in the Vale of Pickering.

The first mention of Heslerton in the historical record is when the township of the same name appears in Domesday Book compiled around the year 1086, just after the Norman Conquest. By this time, the Anglo-Saxon settlement site was no longer occupied and settlement had probably shifted to the site of the nearby village of West Heslerton. It is usual for settlements of this size to last for a few hundred years and then gradually die out as settlement shifts to another location.

36 The western edge of the Wolds from the surrounding lowlands

For larger more important settlements, occupation appears to have remained intact for much longer periods. The earliest historical records give us a glimpse of the location of the larger settlements of East Yorkshire. Those that emerge in the Middle Ages as significant centres are all situated evenly around the edges of the Wolds (3). Domesday Book singles out both Pocklington and Beverley as the only places in the region where officially licensed traders could operate. The town of Driffield may have origins before the Norman Conquest as Bede mentions the name as the place where King Aldfrith died in 705. At this time, the name Driffield probably refers to an estate used by the royal house of Northumbria rather than a town. There are many Anglo-Saxon burials from the west of the modern town. Beverley was a regionally important trading and commercial centre during the twelfth to fourteenth centuries but began as a religious centre in the Anglo-Saxon period based around the shrine of St John. Market Weighton on the western side of the Wolds emerges as a market centre in the Middle Ages but may have importance before the Norman Conquest. Very close by is the village of Goodmanham where Bede recalled the overturning of the pagan shrine at the time of the conversion of the Anglo-Saxon royal house to Christianity. By implication one of Edwin's royal residences must have been located close by. Finally, the town of Malton on the north-western corner of the Wolds had been an important Roman centre and later was used in the Viking period and beyond as a commercial and market centre. We know that these places located evenly around the edge of the Wolds were significant commercial and administrative centres during the Middle Ages because of the body of historical evidence that grows after the eleventh century. The origins of these places depend on much more fragmentary evidence from both archaeology and documents dating from before the Norman Conquest.

EARLY MEDIEVAL ESTATES

At the end of the Roman period, it is not clear what happened to the settlement pattern. We know that the Roman towns of East Yorkshire do not survive in the same form beyond the fifth century. Some of them may continue to have been used as agricultural centres or even as the residences of the rich and powerful in post Roman society. The late Roman economy based on markets and towns changed to a system based on rural agriculture organised around a patchwork of quasi tribal groups rooted to certain specific areas. In the post Roman period a system of rural estates with their origins in the increasingly rural late Roman economy was probably the basis for the settlement pattern. These estates are not historically recorded until vague references start to appear in the eleventh century. However, by this time they had begun to fragment and fall apart and so it is very difficult to build up any clear picture of them. For this reason, many historians actually question whether the estates existed at all. The estates were not recorded before the eleventh century and after that time there are two strands of evidence that can be used to identify the estate centres and their constituent settlements. The 'minster' or 'mother' churches recorded in the eleventh to thirteenth centuries are likely to have been based at places which already had a role as a territorial centre. These same places, like Pocklington, Weaverthorpe, Driffield and Bridlington are also recorded in Domesday Book as having a number of dependent settlements attached to them (37).

The 'multiple estate' was the term given to these agrarian territories by Glanville Jones, although their existence is by no means universally accepted. They have been recognised in northeast England, West Yorkshire, Wales and Scotland in the early medieval period. These rural estates were based on a number of interdependent settlements, which owed duties and obligations to a main settlement or *caput*. Very often these central places emerged as administrative or ecclesiastical centres in the medieval period. Domesday Book recorded some of the archaic dependencies and links between settlements. The individual

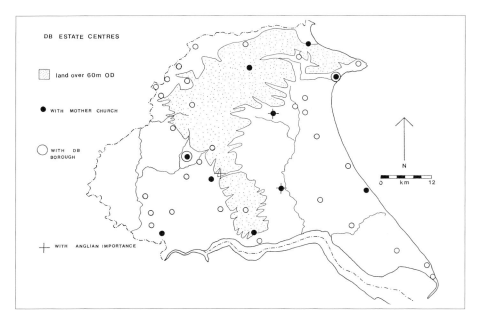

37 Probable estate centres for which *sokelands* and *berewicks* were recorded by Domesday Book. This may suggest a network of rural estates in the post Roman period. These centres tended to concentrate around the edges of the Wolds and correlate closely with the sites of mother churches from the early medieval period

settlements dependent on the estate centre were often described as *berewick* or *sokeland* to that place. This hierarchy and dependency had largely become redundant by the eleventh century as the old estates had become fragmented.

It is not possible to create a map of these estates as a patchwork of neat bounded territories. The evidence is not there and in any case this may not be how the system worked. What we can do is identify a series of places all located around the edge of the Wolds, which consistently display evidence for an early territorial centre (*37*). This role probably originated from before the Norman Conquest. The distribution of the estate centres around the edges of the Wolds may tell us something about the way they worked and indeed about the nature of the Wolds landscape at this time.

One of the main characteristics of these estates from elsewhere in the country is that they usually contained an area dedicated to pasture. This was often an extensive tract of higher or marginal ground that could be used by communities attached to the estate as common pasture. It differed from the idea of commons in the medieval township systems as by the Middle Ages, the pastures were usually restricted to single townships. The estate pastures, were much larger and open for use by many neighbouring communities. There

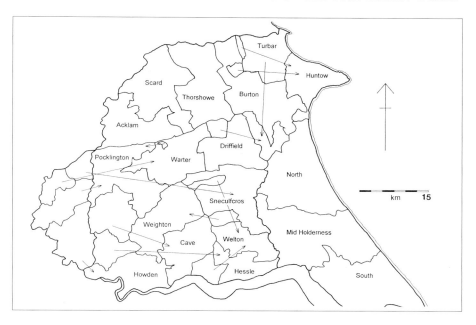

38 East Yorkshire hundreds as they were recorded in the Domesday Book. Many hundreds had detached dependencies in other parts of the Riding. These are marked with arrows. *Information from Faull and Stinson* 1987

are examples of such pastures across the north of England recorded in various eleventh- and twelfth-century documents. Some good examples come from the Church estates in Northumberland where these areas are often referred to as *shire moor*.

The common pasture known as *Huntow* lay inland from Bridlington and stretched across the boundaries of several adjacent townships on the high Wold land above the town. It is recorded in documents as late as 1771 but the name must go back as far as the eleventh century. *Huntow* was also the name for the early medieval administrative territory or 'hundred' to which the townships in this area belonged at the time of Domesday Book (*38*). The pasture itself extended across the boundaries of the townships of Speeton, Buckton and Grindale. In each township, the piece of pasture was always known as *Huntow* and this rather suggests that the pasture pre-dates the township boundaries. These places are all recorded in Domesday Book as *sokelands* of Bridlington, dependent settlements owing archaic render and allegiance to the major settlement. It is echoes like this preserved in the documents of the eleventh century that may be telling us about an earlier system of estates, already in decay by this time (*51*). In this case, the centre of the estate would have lain at Bridlington and the pasture of *Huntow* would have provided common grazing for the communities who belonged to this estate. It is surely not coincidental that Bridlington also housed a mother church or minster in the early medieval period whose large parish included many of the *sokeland* settlements.

THE WOLDS VILLAGES

For the East Yorkshire estates with their centres distributed evenly around the edge of the Wolds, it would make perfect sense if they used the high chalkland as a landscape of extensive pasture. We will see in the next chapter how all sorts of historical evidence from the medieval township system may support this claim. But first we need to consider the villages of the Wolds. We need to know when these settlements originated and whether we can see a difference between the Wolds villages and those that cluster around the wold-edges. The origins of villages are difficult to trace. Archaeology only really works in those examples, which were abandoned and now occupy green field sites as they can be excavated and surveyed.

One such example was the deserted medieval village of Wharram Percy. This settlement was abandoned during the fifteenth century but was excavated thoroughly over many years beginning in 1948. Today, the site contains a ruined church, a small cluster of farm cottages, a large pond and a series of earthworks related to medieval house plots and holloways (*colour plates 10* and *11*). It is a picturesque spot. The digging took place in the summer months and was staffed by volunteers, students and even borstal boys on some occasions. It became an institution for those who got involved and created a family of archaeologists who all fondly remember their annual get-together. The results of the excavations showed that the village flourished between the twelfth and fifteenth centuries. Each domestic plot occupied an enclosure, which stretched back from the village street. The layout of these was so regular that they were probably laid out according to a plan. One of the surprises from the excavations was the discovery that the settlement had been long-lived, comprising evidence of Anglo-Saxon, Roman and even Iron Age remains. No one is sure whether this occupation was continuous without a break between the Iron Age and medieval periods. The best way to look at this sequence is probably to say that the site contained small-scale farmsteads until the tenth to twelfth century when a much larger settlement was planned and laid out.

It would be easy to argue that villages all over the Wolds parallel this pattern of continuity. Only very few have been abandoned and even fewer have been studied archaeologically in the same detail as Wharram Percy. If the sequence

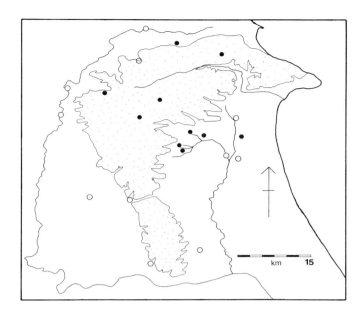

39 Early Old English place-names on the Wolds and wold-edge. Those names using the *ham* element are open circles while those seen by Gelling as early topographic names such as Eastburn, Kirkburn, Sledmere and Fimber are marked as solid dots

at Wharram is representative, the Wolds has been occupied and settled more or less continuously since the Iron Age. But can the Wharram sequence be found elsewhere? The first thing to say is that its location is not typical of Wolds villages. For a start, it has access to fresh spring water and is found not in the interior of the Wolds but on its north-western edge. Although the village lies on the chalk, its situation may indicate it has more in common with wold-edge sites than those in the heart of the Wolds.

PLACE NAMES

In order to resolve this question, it is important to look beyond Wharram to the rest of the settlement pattern. Firstly, we need to examine the origins of the existing villages and secondly we should gather the archaeological evidence for settlements here during the Anglo-Saxon period. You can get a generalised idea of the antiquity of a settlement pattern by looking at its place names. Most of the names of East Yorkshire villages were coined between the seventh and eleventh centuries AD. The majority of the names contain Old English or Scandinavian elements although a small number were named in the twelfth to thirteenth century with characteristic Norman French words. Very few villages in East Yorkshire or even England have names that date from the Roman period or before. This may be because the settlement pattern altered so much after

40 The place names indicate a long history of settlement

the Roman occupation but also because the language used by the country's inhabitants changed drastically between the sixth and ninth centuries. Whilst we should not use the place name of a village to determine the date of origin for that specific settlement, it is useful to get a generalised pattern across a wider area by looking at the distribution of the names and their relative ages (*40*).

The first port of call is the detailed inventory and analysis of East Yorkshire place names by E.H. Smith. Although this was published in 1937 it remains a very useful source of reference. I have also used an unpublished article on the Wolds place names written by Margaret Gelling, who is probably the foremost place name scholar in the country. Gelling's paper was inspired by the archaeological work at Wharram and she tried to set the history of this village within a broader regional context of settlement development. She concluded that the names on the edge of the Wolds tended to be earlier than those in the heart of the chalkland and this suggests that there may have been some settlement expansion onto the Wolds between the ninth and eleventh centuries.

The earliest group of names were probably coined in the seventh century. They used Old English terms and referred to topographic features in the landscape rather than names for farms or settlements. A typical group occurs on the eastern dip slope of the Wolds close to Driffield. There is a cluster of names such as Eastburn, Southburn and Kirkburn that all use the word *burn*, an Old English term meaning 'stream'. The name of a neighbouring village, Elmswell can also be traced back to this early phase of naming in the seventh century

(39). For Gelling these are some of the oldest names in East Yorkshire. Eastburn, Southburn and Elmswell were abandoned as settlements in the post-medieval period but Kirkburn has survived probably because it housed the parish church for all three settlements.

Another place name element that belongs to the earliest phase of Old English naming appears in names such as Goodmanham and Yedingham. The *ham* term means a farm or hamlet and again these names are distributed around the edges of the Wolds and never found in its interior. In contrast to this distribution, there are many later names using *tun, by* and *thorp* that are scattered throughout East Yorkshire including the interior of the Wolds. The *tun* element appears in places such as Garton, Malton and North Dalton and although these names are English in origin, Gelling sees them as later than the eighth century. The Scandinavian names using *by* and *thorp* such as Fridaythorpe and Tibthorpe must be later than the ninth century when Scandinavian language spread through the area. By the tenth century, East Yorkshire was being ruled by Scandinavian kings based in York and this political takeover must have been accompanied by new landlords and changes to landholding in the more remote areas of the region away from bustling Jorvik. It is in this environment, that new settlements were founded on the Wolds as estates were broken up and pieces of land handed out to new Scandinavian landlords.

SETTLEMENT ARCHAEOLOGY

The place names can help us to see the development of settlement patterns but should not be used to trace the origins of specific individual settlements. The origins of each village can be discovered in the archaeological remains of houses, middens, trackways and boundaries that lie buried beneath the modern high streets and village greens. However, these are busy inhabited places and cannot be turned into open area archaeological digs at the drop of a hat. The Wharram Percy example shows what can be achieved on village sites that have been abandoned but surviving villages are expanding and thriving. Since 1989, archaeology has been a formal part of the planning process so that any construction in these villages will be monitored, to ensure that archaeological remains may be recovered from the affected site. But more often than not, these are small-scale investigations in areas where successive generations of building and occupation have already destroyed any trace of earlier habitation. Most of the good archaeological sites are found away from modern villages in agricultural land where aerial photographs or geophysical survey can pinpoint sites before they are actually excavated. This does not help with our quest to discover the origins of the modern Wolds villages.

If we gather together all the archaeological evidence for the period between the end of the Roman occupation (fifth century) and the Norman Conquest (1066) there are some clear and obvious patterns that may help. Much of this evidence was unearthed in the nineteenth and earlier twentieth century and many finds were made by chance during construction work or quarrying so we should be careful about drawing too many conclusions from them. The only excavations from this period undertaken with modern archaeological techniques in the northern half of the Wolds are Wharram Percy, West Heslerton, Sewerby, Cottam and Thwing (11). The site at Wharram Percy was occupied during the (later) Anglo-Saxon period but on a much smaller scale to the site at West Heslerton where an extensive settlement thrived alongside its cemetery between the fifth and seventh centuries. The excavations at Sewerby were in the grounds of Sewerby Hall on the east coast near Bridlington. They revealed traces of a large Anglo-Saxon cemetery. The sites at Cottam and Thwing are different. Both are fairly close to one another on the high Wolds east of Sledmere. At Cottam there was a small but wealthy settlement, which was occupied between the ninth and tenth centuries. It produced many fine pieces of metalwork and must have been the residence, possibly a hunting lodge, of a wealthy and probably powerful local landlord. Thwing is an interesting site for it began life as a late Bronze Age hill fort, which may itself have been sited on a Neolithic henge monument. It was re-used between the seventh and tenth centuries again as a high-status residence. Neither of these latter two sites are regular everyday settlements like West Heslerton or Wharram. They must have belonged to elite groups in Anglo-Saxon society and may not reflect the wider settlement pattern inhabited by small rural communities who made a living off the land. Apart from these sites, the remains of actual settlements are very rare. Where they do exist they have always been found on the wold-edges along the margins of the chalkland close to water supplies and a varied range of agricultural land. This is just the kind of location occupied by the site at West Heslerton.

There are burial sites from this period scattered across the Wolds and the wold-edges. Some of these are single graves, discovered by chance or during small-scale excavations, whilst others are full cemeteries. Burials have been found alongside many of the modern villages strung out along the western edges of the Wolds beneath the steep escarpment. There are cemeteries known from Londesbrough, Newbald and Nunburnholme along the western wold-edge. It seems likely that that these lay alongside settlements that now lie buried beneath the modern village. The same is true for the villages around Rudston, Harpham and Nafferton on the eastern edge of the Wolds north of Driffield. Indeed Nafferton has produced traces of settlement from this period.

The situation in the interior of the Wolds appears to have been very different. All the burials found here have been inserted into earlier monuments such as

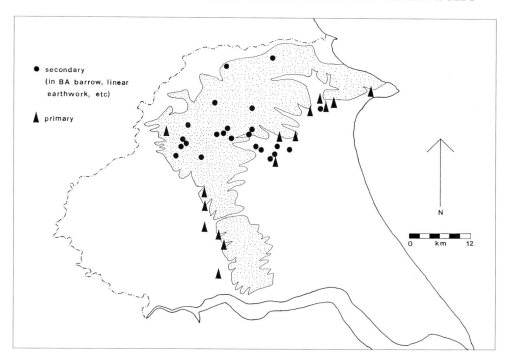

41 Anglo-Saxon burials showing how secondary graves (made in round barrows or linear earthworks) were almost always located on the Wolds. In contrast, the flat cemeteries around the wold-edge probably lay close to settlements. The secondary burials on the Wolds suggest that the chalklands were seen as different from the wold-edge and lowlands between the sixth and ninth centuries AD

round barrows or the banks of linear earthworks. As we will see in the next chapter, these burials are likely to have been deliberately placed away from the areas of settlement in places that held fear and mystery for the communities living around the wold-edge (*41*).

The wold-edge villages nestling under the steep slopes of the escarpment can be traced back to the medieval period but their origins may extend further back in time. These village sites are surrounded by archaeological remains from the Anglo-Saxon and Roman periods and many of the villages have names that were coined as early as the seventh century. Areas around places like Rudston, Newbald, Heslerton and Driffield are favoured settlement areas where communities probably lived continuously throughout the first millennium AD. That is not to say that the same settlement sites were occupied without a break but that settlements shifted around the neighbourhood throughout this time before becoming fixed between the ninth and eleventh centuries.

What of the villages up on the chalk and away from the wold-edges and the low-lying vales? We know that most of these existed in the eleventh century for they are named in the Domesday Book. The place names are generally using late Old English and Scandinavian terms and these probably date from the ninth century onwards. The work at Wharram Percy showed that this village was probably planned around the tenth century as part of a massive re-organisation of landholding and settlement in this area. These radical changes may coincide with the takeover of land by new Scandinavian landlords. Elsewhere on the Wolds, there are signs that the medieval open fields were also laid out at this time as grand acts of landscape design. The historical records appear to suggest that the arable strips stretched out from one township boundary to the next. In an occupied landscape, you would have thought this could only be possible where a new landowning power was able to ruthlessly impose their will on a rural population, ignoring the intricate byways of lanes and field plots. On the other hand, if the Wolds landscape was largely un-occupied then it would be far easier to impose such radical agrarian plans onto it.

We shall see in the next chapter how the historical sources from the medieval period and later may contain echoes of the character of this landscape before the Norman Conquest. As settlement and agriculture encroached onto the Wolds between the ninth and eleventh centuries, the layout and look of the landscape changed drastically but not suddenly. The changes could have occurred over two hundred years and marginal land was still being appropriated and taken in to cultivation as late as the twelfth century. The Wolds of the thirteenth century was a very different place to that of the ninth but the old landscape of open spaces and pasture was never fully erased. Some of the trackways and pastures survived into the Middle Ages and are vaguely recorded in the medieval landscape. In the eighth century, the Wolds would have been a place of mystery and difference to those communities living round its edges. Here resided the spirits of the dead inhabiting remote valleys. The strange mounds and banks spoke of ancient communities and sometimes these were used for burying the unwanted dead. A traveller passing from Newbald to Driffield would have used the long winding tracks that crossed the Wolds but would have done so hurriedly. They would have passed by herders and flocks and the odd itinerant or outsider for whom these wild open spaces were home. Small settlements may have existed up here but the place was not the same as the rich hearty farmland down in the lowland vales.

SIX

IN SEARCH OF THE PASTORAL WOLDS

In chapter five, we outlined some of the problems and questions surrounding the post Roman period on the Wolds. Was this place inhabited? Where are the remains of settlements? Was the Wolds landscape different to the surrounding lowlands and if so, why? What was this landscape used for and what was its character? In this chapter we shall try and answer some of these questions more fully with clues found within medieval and post-medieval documents.

I began to think about the character of the post-Roman Wolds when I read an article by Harold Fox about areas of wold land elsewhere in the country. He talked about the pastoral heritage of these areas and argued that the people of the Wolds enjoyed a common personality evident in the distinctive character of their landscapes. He suggested that these landscapes were used as pastures during the pre-Norman centuries and that they had become colonised and occupied in the centuries leading up to the time of Domesday Book in the late eleventh century. He described his idea of a typical wold landscape as follows:

A stranger coming into a wold one evening in the seventh century or the eighth would have entered a wood pasture… a landscape dominated by those two types of land-use rather than by ploughland. He would have seen clumps of wood casting long shadows over the great open spaces and, everywhere on the pastures, domestic animals of all kinds. Now people come into view, the keepers of those animals returning to their summer dwellings as night closed in. Everywhere traces of older landscapes, all the stranger in the evening light, showed that people had been there before in times long distant even in the seventh century, had buried their dead there, and divided up the land.

Fox had not looked in detail at the Yorkshire Wolds but the evidence appears to bear him out. The historical evidence presented below has identified a system of long-distance trackways running across this landscape, as well as a patchwork of pastures, some of which survived in to the medieval period. Between the sixth and ninth centuries this was an un-claimed remote landscape of extensive pastures and tracks.

TRACKWAYS AND TOWNSHIP BOUNDARIES

With this image in mind one day I drove from Sheffield to spend a day walking and searching out some of the sites where echoes of this landscape may be visible. My first stop was at the Sykes monument on the road between Sledmere and Garton (*70* and *71*). I knew about the history of the ornate stone spire, which was raised as a memorial to Sir Tatton Sykes in the 1860s. It is well known to archaeologists, as Anglo-Saxon skeletons were unearthed during the building work allowing Mortimer to discover a linear cemetery of burials that had been placed along the ditch of a much older linear earthwork (*52*). I had come to look at the site and to examine two areas alongside the road where the prehistoric earthwork still survived. To the east there were three parallel banks and ditches that turned a tight corner at the head of a dramatic dry valley. The single ditch of this earthwork continued along the upper side of the valley and was clearly visible winding its way off into the distance. To the west there were more massive earthwork banks preserved in the nearby plantation of Black Wood. I spoke to the woodman that worked for the Sledmere estate and he explained how they made life difficult for him for the law protected them, as they were ancient monuments.

I began to walk along the track between the fields. This grassy strip stretched out for miles across the landscape to the south-west and although the linear earthwork was no longer visible, it looked from the maps I had that it had originally followed the same line as the grassy track. The landscape here is rolling country and is characteristic of the eastern dip slope of the Wolds. The track, which is here known as the Green Lane, ran along a ridge on the north side of the broad open valley of Wetwang Slack. Down in the base of the valley was the site of the Iron Age cemetery and settlement excavated in the 1980s (*27*). The track went on and on as if it was much older than the surrounding fields but it was obviously no longer used by traffic other than tractors and walkers.

At one point, the grassy strip ran out and it looked as though the lane had ended. However, a sign marking the way as a public footpath pointed across an unmarked field, continuing the course of the track. The right of way was all that had survived at this point. The rest of the track, its hedges and broad grass baulk, had been ploughed into the field. After a few fields I came across the main road between Wetwang and Fridaythorpe (72). On the other side of the road, the right of way continued and it was again running along a track, this time the access road to Holmfield Farm. After the farm the track continued until it joined the head of Holm Dale and carried on as a straight stretch of trackway before merging with the main road. Here the right of way finally ran out. I had left the car at Sykes Monument and had to retrace my steps all the way back, a distance of about 7km.

Back at the car, I studied the OS map and the route I had taken stood out as an unbroken line sweeping across the landscape. This route had intrigued me. In the modern landscape it was a little-used right of way but had continued for several miles between the modern fields. These fields were only as old as enclosure, eighteenth- or nineteenth-century, but seemed to have been laid out around the trackway. It was also curious that the track was followed by modern parish boundaries for most of its course. How far back in time did this feature go and how had it survived for so long?

The Green Lane turned out to be a very ancient feature that had probably been used in this landscape as trackway and boundary since before 1000 BC. This track had also been used as a long-distance route during the Anglo-Saxon period. Long trackways such as this were a feature of the post Roman Wolds in other areas. This was a tell-tale signal that Harold Fox's ideas of the post Roman Wolds having been an uninhabited pasture, may well apply here in East Yorkshire.

A few weeks later, I had the chance to go to the map collection of the Brynmor Jones Library in Hull and spent a couple of days pouring over maps of the Wolds from the eighteenth and nineteenth centuries. Before the mid-nineteenth century there were few detailed maps but there was one very useful example surveyed by Thomas Jeffreys in 1771. The layout of villages and roads that appears on this map was more or less the same as it is today apart from a road that ran unhindered from Bridlington in the east all the way to the western edge of the Wolds near Fridaythorpe. This road turned out to be the same Green Lane that I had walked along. Another map of the area by Warburton, dated to the mid-eighteenth century, seemed to back this up (42). He too had marked a long-distance routeway striking out across this part of the Wolds and passing between the villages of Fridaythorpe and Wetwang. The track did not seem to be connecting local villages but tended to avoid the settlements. Why was this? During the eighteenth century, coach roads were laid out across much of the

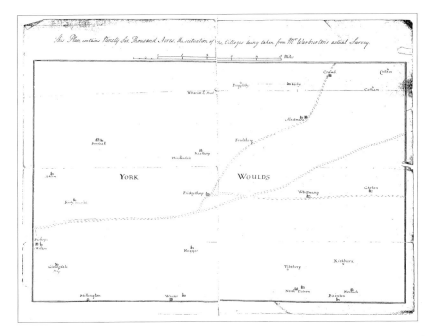

42 Warburton's map of roads and villages on the central Wolds dating from the mid-eighteenth century. The Sledmere Green Lane runs across the map from east to west passing between the villages of Fridaythorpe and Wetwang (DDSY/106/8). *Courtesy Brynmor Jones Library, University of Hull*

English landscape and perhaps that is what the Green Lane was. A route for fast horse-drawn mail coaches connecting Bridlington with York would not have needed to pass through local villages on its way.

The Green Lane had been used as an eighteenth-century coach road but why was it followed by parish boundaries for most of its course? Modern parishes are civil territories used as the most local level of administration in local government. They are based on the much more ancient system of ecclesiastical parishes which had sprung out of the more localised pattern of townships. Townships were generally small territories of land that surrounded medieval villages whilst ecclesiastical parishes were territories served by a parish church. The origins of townships go back to at least the eleventh century when they were units of land, which supported a self-sufficient agrarian community. The village was where this community lived but in the Middle Ages they belonged to the township. The names given in Domesday Book (1086) are not describing actual settlements but township territories. The modern parish boundaries followed by the Green Lane had originally been the boundaries of townships but which came first: The lane or the boundaries?

I produced a map of townships for the central Wolds using the boundaries marked on the 1854 Ordnance Survey maps and it showed some interesting

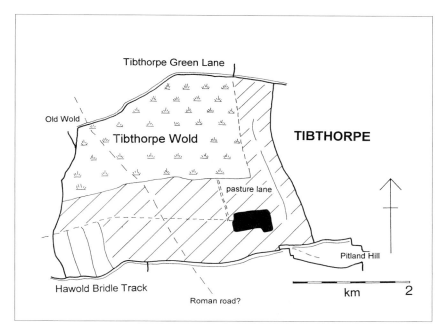

43 Township map of Tibthorpe as it was at enclosure in 1796. The pasture of Tibthorpe Wold was clearly marked on the enclosure map and was probably carved in from more extensive pasture zones around the time of the Norman Conquest. The northern and southern boundaries were marked by long distance east–west trackways across the Wolds

patterns (*47*). Most striking of these was the strong continuous line striking through the heart of the pattern. This was the course of the Green Lane. It was not only visible in the stretch between Fridaythorpe and Garton but also to the east around Rudston and Kilham. For the township boundaries to follow the lane so consistently it must mean the Green Lane was older than the townships. These territories are at least as old as the eleventh century and their boundaries here must have followed an existing trackway or boundary.

There were other continuous lines within the township pattern similar to that followed by the Sledmere Green Lane. One ran in parallel to it along the southern edge of the townships of North Dalton and Huggate. Another continuous boundary ran north to south down the central spine of the chalk Wolds. I went back to the bigger scale maps and saw that this second continuous boundary was also followed by a right of way all the way from the springs of Eastburn on the eastern dip slope to the springs of Millington on the western wold-edge. I walked the whole route at the next opportunity and found that this route did not run along a broad grassy lane but simply followed hedge-lines. The track ran along the bottom of a dry valley called Deep Dale and then up onto the central watershed of the Wolds where you can see for miles in both directions.

It then continued downhill and skirted round the heads of two very steep side dry valleys above the village of Warter before ending up on the scarp edge and heading down a dry valley to the village and springs of Millington (*48*).

We now had two east–west boundaries that both held rights of way and appeared to be older than the townships to either side (*47*). Another north–south line also formed part of this primary arrangement of boundaries. These boundaries must have already existed before the townships were laid out but when was this? The townships were at least as old as the tenth century. The earliest land charter from East Yorkshire comes from Newbald and describes the boundaries of ecclesiastical land here in 963. Up on the Wold, the boundary followed a series of landmarks such as notable trees, trackways, barrows and banks whilst down at the base of the scarp it ran along streams and field boundaries. It is possible to trace this tenth-century boundary in the modern landscape and it seems to have followed the same course as the medieval township boundary. This suggests that the township was based on this pre-Norman estate.

The earliest township maps are the enclosure maps of the later eighteenth and early nineteenth century. These were drawn up when the lands belonging to each township were enclosed and taken from collective management into private ownership. It was at this time the regular rectangular fields of the Wolds were laid out and the short hawthorn hedges were planted. New roads too were designed with broad grassy verges. These maps are sometimes very good sources for the layout of the landscape before enclosure and they often illustrate the routes of early trackways and open fields.

The maps for North Dalton and Tibthorpe opened up several new avenues for research, revealing more about the Wolds in the post Roman centuries. The first thing that these maps showed was the existence of a hitherto lost township called *Howard* or *Hawold* and this led to the recognition of other similar small territories which had survived but whose origins were obscure. Secondly these two maps started to show where the dedicated pasture areas lay in the medieval period and it became clear that these pastures had originally been carved out of more extensive grazing grounds that originated from before the Norman Conquest.

Each enclosure map deals specifically with a single township but the names of neighbouring townships are given, written around the edge of the territory alongside the boundary line. On the North Dalton map the neighbouring township to the north was not Huggate as expected but a territory called *Howard*. Similarly along the south-western edge of Tibthorpe township was the name *Hawold* (*55*). These two names obviously referred to the same place that lay in the south-eastern corner of what was now Huggate township. *Hawold* or *Howard* appears to have been another township, which has since given its name to the modern farm, Haywold. This township had obviously ceased to be

44 A winter landscape south of Wetwang. The Tibthorpe Green Lane can be seen as a line of trees and bushes running across the picture in the middle distance

recognised by the time the 1854 OS map was surveyed but some memory of it had survived at the time of enclosure (*46*). It was not clear when this township originated or whether it had ever contained a settlement. The name *Hawold* or *Houwald* is mentioned in several twelfth- and thirteenth-century charters and in 1872 Kelly's Directory records that, 'It was originally a grange of the abbey of Watton and is exempt from tithes'.

The northern boundary of Tibthorpe township was also known as the Green Lane and still carries this name even on modern maps (*43*). On the ground a wooded lane marks this boundary and this lane continues eastwards towards Elmswell and Driffield on the eastern wold-edge. In places it is a broad grassy strip and in others simply a right of way alongside the edge of a field. I walked the wooded part of the route passing along the northern edge of Tibthorpe township. At Beadygraves, the modern boundaries trace a vicious and confusing dogleg but it seems that the older lines were much smoother (*44* and *45*). Maybe there had been disputes about the exact course of the boundaries here causing the old continuous lines to be re-drawn. At the point where the Tibthorpe boundary should give way to the old boundary of *Hawold* township, the wooded lane suddenly stopped. At this point walkers are directed out from the overgrown shade of the Tibthorpe Green Lane and along the edge of an enclosure field to the south (*colour plates 21*

Above left: 45 Walking down the Tibthorpe Green Lane where it marks the boundary between Wetwang and Tibthorpe townships

Above right: 46 Haywold is now a link in the chain of industrialised pig production. It was a small township in its own right which was originally a grange belonging to Watton Priory. The name originates from *Houwald* and names like this were probably given to the wide expanses of open pasture here in the Anglo-Saxon period

and *22*). In Jeffrey's time, this lane continued straight across this field but any trace of it has now been lost and ploughed up. The loss of this boundary and the track that followed it must be linked to the loss of the township of *Hawold* when it was incorporated into the wider territory of Huggate.

I had made two important discoveries from the enclosure maps. Firstly I had found a small lost township called something like *Hawold* or *Howard*. In doing so, and locating its boundary, another long-distance trackway had come to light. This was another Green Lane and ran from the wold-edge near Eastburn into the heart of the high wolds and then seemed to join up with the north–south ridgeway (*47* and *48*).

So on this part of the Wolds there was a series of very old trackways that ran across the chalkland from east to west. They seemed to be earlier than the township boundaries and their lines had survived well in the modern landscape.

Before the townships existed, these tracks must have been the main features of this landscape. The overall pattern of tracks takes account of the topography of the Wolds. They tend to follow ridges or valleys and avoid the steep slopes of the dry valleys.

OLD PASTURES

The early medieval landscape was starting to look very different from the medieval countryside of villages and fields. What is more, there were echoes of this earlier pre-Norman landscape like the trackways that had survived beyond the eleventh century and were still visible in today's countryside. But what was this landscape being used for before the township boundaries existed when the trackways were in use? Was it inhabited and how was it farmed? Were the modern villages around at this time?

A clue came again from the enclosure maps. In the Middle Ages, each township territory contained arable fields, which were huge swathes of cultivated land divided up into strips. The layout of these fields was sometimes marked on enclosure maps. The medieval arable fields were called 'open fields' because they were not subdivided by boundaries. Townships usually contained between two and four such fields and in several cases on the Wolds these fields stretched from one boundary to another filling the township area. During the medieval period the land was farmed according to collective co-operative principles using a mixture of arable and pastoral regimes. In those townships where the open fields filled the territory there was usually one field left fallow where animals could graze. For instance the townships of Garton and Fimber were filled with arable lands whilst the land within Wetwang township had one small area devoted to pasture on the southern edge of the territory. In a few townships there were larger designated pastures zones and these were used entirely for grazing. For instance, in Huggate there are two separate pastures (55). One of these was still named Huggate Pasture in the mid-nineteenth century although by that time these lands had all been enclosed into regular hedged fields owned by private individuals. The pastures are often recorded on the enclosure maps. During the Middle Ages they were common pastures for the use of the township community.

Why was it that the pastures existed in some townships but not in others? Was there any patterning to the distribution of these grazing areas? I went through each township in the central Wolds and tried to map the areas of pasture. This showed something very interesting (49). Pasture land was always found on the edge of the township and was linked to another on the other side of the boundary

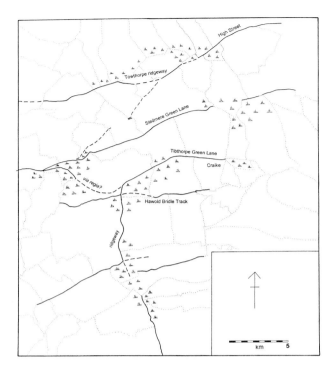

47 The trackways across the post Roman Wolds and their relationship with the township boundaries (dotted lines). The tufts of grass indicate areas of pasture recorded in post medieval documents but probably current throughout the Middle Ages

in the neighbouring township. It was almost like these areas had been carved from a much larger more extensive tract of pasture and divided out amongst the adjacent townships. If this was the case, then as with the trackways the extensive pastures must be older than the townships. They must have been relics from the pastoral Wolds and were also closely related to the long distance trackways.

For Tibthorpe township the pasture was very clearly marked on the enclosure map. It occupied the northern part of the township in the area now known as Tibthorpe Wold (*43*). The northern limit of the pasture was the Tibthorpe Green Lane that also marked its township boundary. On the other side of this boundary was the open field of Wetwang but in the south-western corner of Wetwang was a small area of pasture known as Thorndale. There is no enclosure map to confirm this location but there are useful references to this pasture in historical documents dating from the period of enclosure in the eighteenth century (*60*). The 1854 OS map refers to this area as Old Wold, suggesting it had lain as grassland for many centuries. Elsewhere the same pattern occurs. For instance, the townships that were strung along the Great Wold Valley, lie in strips running across the contours of the valley side. Their pastures were all at the southern end of each township and occupied a broad strip of high ground. The upper slopes of the valley side must have been dedicated to an extensive zone of pasture or waste

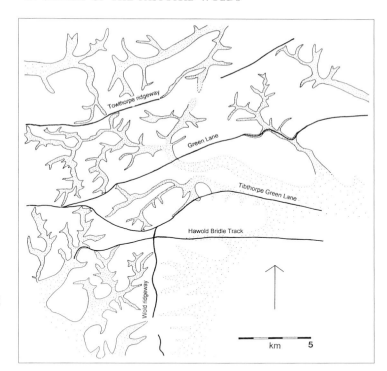

48 Post Roman
tracks showing the
way that they relate
to the pattern of dry
valleys. The tracks tend
to follow ridges and
cross the necks of land
between the valley
heads

from which the townships took their own specific piece of grazing ground.
There were pastures in the north of both Driffield and Elmswell townships and
others in the south of Cottam on the other side of the boundary. Another cluster
of pastures occurred to the west of Huggate (*49*).

The pastures belonging to each township made up larger areas that appeared to
represent the last vestiges of formerly more extensive grazing grounds and these
large pastures must date from before the formation of the townships. There are a
number of discrete pastures that belonged to distant townships and the rights of
these detached territories often survived into the eighteenth century. To the west
of Huggate, there was a small detached piece of Bishop Wilton township known
as Greenwick. This may have been a detached pasture belonging to Bishop
Wilton and is interesting as it was enclosed with ancient banks and ditches.

To the west of here was another smaller detached pasture known as Wetwang
Rakes. There is a very useful map of this tiny territory dated to 1760 (*56*).
Documentary sources record how citizens of Wetwang were able to use this
pasture. Although it was physically separate from Wetwang lands, the lord of the
manor of Wetwang held rights within it under a system of intercommoning. This
was when the occupants of more than one township shared rights of pasture in
the same piece of land. As late as the eighteenth century, Wetwang Rakes was:

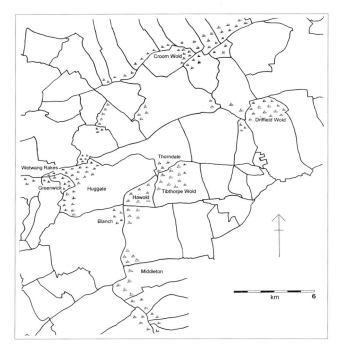

49 The pattern of pastures recorded in the eighteenth- and nineteenth-century documentary sources. Each township appears to have carved its grazing land out of much larger pastures that must pre-date the foundation of these townships

about four miles distant from ye town in Bishop Wilton township .... There is no close belonging to it, and ye land is about 120 acres. The town of Bishop Wilton claim the right of intercommoning (with cows only) as also threaten ye tenant of my lords to stint him to 140 sheep which at present I find he keeps 300 upon ....

These are echoes of the pastoral heritage of the Wolds suggesting that this area around Greenwick, Wetwang Rakes and west Huggate had been pasture for a very long time. At some point, probably around the time the township boundaries were being laid out the rights to these pastures were divided up amongst the township communities. The townships that contained designated pastures in the Middle Ages appeared to have taken these grazing areas in from what were originally much larger tracts of pasture land.

LAND GRANTS AND MONASTIC GRANGES

During the twelfth and thirteenth centuries, it was common for individual landowners to give land to monasteries or the Church, not only as a gesture of spiritual insurance but also as a display of social power. Much of the evidence for the nature of land at this time comes from little details hidden away in these

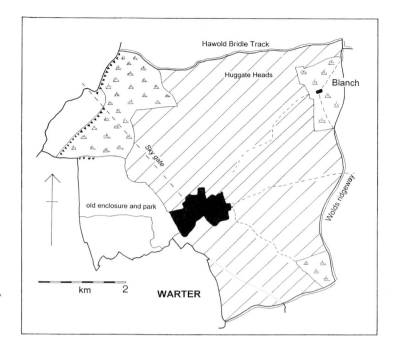

50 The township of Warter showing Blanch Farm in the north-east of the township. This was the site of a 'shieling', a seasonal pastoral base, in the early Middle Ages

grants. They describe how the high ground of the Wolds was being divided up and partitioned out amongst the priories and abbeys of the region.

Much of this high ground in the central Wolds was still marginal in the twelfth and thirteenth centuries and the boundaries were still being laid out at this time. This land had previously been largely uninhabited and only loosely claimed. The process of apportionment was slow and gradual. The boundaries between townships were not always fixed immediately and in many cases there are hints in the documentary sources that a fuzzy tenurial zone existed at the margins between the two territories. It is these areas that were likely to have once been more extensive pasture zones. A quote from a document dated to 1539 describes the practice of common vicinage where:

> the waste ground of two tonships lye together, and noother hedge nor pale betweene to kepe their catel asunder, so that the catel of one township goth over his meire or bounde into the waste ground of the other towne….

In the north-eastern corner of Warter township, there is an isolated farm called Blanch. This name first appears in a land grant of 1156, which deals with land being given to Meaux Abbey for a grange (*50*). The land had previously been called *Arras* or *Erghes*, meaning 'shieling'. A shieling was a Scandinavian term for a temporary settlement related to seasonal pasture and fits well with this idea of the Wolds acting as pasture at a distance from the permanent settlements. The grant talks about 'all the land of Herghes which is now called Blanch' and describes it as lying 'between Dalton and Warter'. The use of the word 'between' here must imply that the boundary between these two territories was not yet fully fixed in 1156. Another land charter from 1263 records the grant of land, 'upon the new improvement of the wald in Huggate'.

Much of this high central Wolds land was given out to monasteries for granges between the twelfth and fourteenth centuries. The territory of *Hawold* was part of a grange attached to Watton Priory and alongside this land in North Dalton township was another grange belonging to Meaux Abbey (*49*). Others are known from Octon and Burton Fleming also on the high Wolds. Granges like these were farms managed by groups of monks and often based around sheep farming. They were situated on land that had previously been uncultivated and marginal.

As time went on, I was beginning to build a picture of the early medieval Wolds landscape. Evidence from different historical sources suggested that this land was gradually being apportioned out, taken in to cultivation, enclosed and divided between the tenth and thirteenth centuries. The pre-Norman landscape of extensive pastures and long-distance tracks was slowly being eaten away by expanding settlement and farming. The intake of land for granges was probably the end of this process as it focused on the most marginal land on the highest most remote spots on the Wolds. During the process of encroachment townships were laid out and villages founded within them. The interesting thing about this was that it was very similar to what had happened on the Wolds during the later Iron Age. Then too an open pastoral landscape crossed by trackways had given way gradually to a landscape that was enclosed and divided with boundaries, farmed and inhabited by permanent settlements.

LOST TOWNSHIPS AND TERRITORIES

There were some small territories like Hawold, Burrow or Greenwick that appeared never to have contained any settlements of any permanence or size. Some survived into the nineteenth century, whilst others disappeared but were still known in the eighteenth century when they were shown on enclosure maps. What were these little territories and how had they survived for so long with apparently little purpose? They had several elements in common that may hold the clue to their origins. Firstly they were often used as pastures during the Middle Ages and secondly they were surrounded by linear earthworks.

Greenwick was a detached piece of land belonging to Bishop Wilton. It lay alongside another piece of detached pasture known as Wetwang Rakes (*49, 53* and *55*). Both of these small territories were bounded by linear earthworks; banks and ditches presumed to be prehistoric. The southern edge of Greenwick was actually bordered by Huggate Dykes, one of the most impressive of these earthworks on the Wolds with up to six parallel banks and ditches. The township of Burrow lay on the high ground north of Cottam on the watershed ridge that marks the southern edge of the Great Wold Valley (*49*). It was recorded on the enclosure map for Cottam dated 1848. The name survives today as Burrow House Farm in Cottam parish alongside the main road between Sledmere and Bridlington. The territory was defined by the course of steep, dry valleys and on the north by the line of the road. The boundary of Burrow was marked by linear earthworks, which are known to have cut through Iron Age square barrows dating the boundary to the middle Iron Age or later. Aldro was located in the north-west Wolds near to Thixendale. It was defined by dry valleys, which are also followed by linear earthworks. Part of this territory is still known as Vessey Pasture and was used for grazing throughout the Middle Ages. The territories of Greenwick, Burrow, Hawold and Aldro have much in common. They did not contain settlements; dry valleys surrounded them; and linear earthworks marked their boundaries. The linears are undated but I wonder whether these territories were actually pieces of pasture carved out of the extensive grazing grounds sometime between the ninth and eleventh centuries when this area was being gradually occupied and enclosed and shared out between nascent communities. Some of the territories could have re-used linear banks that were already ancient but other linear earthworks may have actually been constructed at this time as visible boundaries to these small territories. By choosing to dig ditches and build up banks, the early medieval builders were creating boundaries that looked similar to others which already ran across the landscape and had been around for longer than anyone could remember. If the territory of Burrow was Anglo-Saxon in origin then it must be related to the site at Cottam where a team from the University of York have unearthed the remains of a high-status occupation site. This site lies within the Burrow township territory.

Most of these territories were enclosed by linear earthworks but they all lay alongside the trackways that crossed the Wolds during the post Roman period. In every case at least one side of the territory was bounded by one of these long-distance tracks (*49*). It seems likely that these territories were enclosed pieces of pasture taken in from the wider expanse of grazing land between the ninth and eleventh centuries. They were then treated as special discrete territories for many centuries, some of them being seen as townships in their own right. Others, like Greenwick,s became detached pieces of other townships.

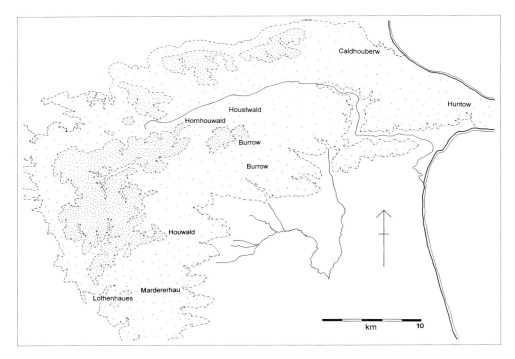

51 The northern Wolds showing names recorded in land grants of the eleventh to thirteenth centuries. These names often using the *wald* and *haugr* elements may have been given to extensive tracts of land before the foundation of townships here

PLACE NAMES IN *HAUGR* AND *WALD*

An element that Burrow, Aldro and Hawold have in common is that their names all use the Old Scandinavian term, *haugr* meaning 'barrow' or 'hill'. In the eleventh century there is a reference to land 'in territorio Houwald' and the earliest reference to Burrow records the name as *Burrehou*. There are many more names that use this term but many have been lost since the twelfth and thirteenth centuries when they appeared in the charters. The medieval land grants were written in Latin and the original documents once held by monasteries and abbeys are preserved in archives and collections throughout the region. Many have been collected together and translated in a very useful series of volumes known as *The Early Yorkshire Charters*. This can be consulted in many libraries across the region. The only way to find what these grants contain is to go through them one by one searching for familiar place names. They contain some interesting patterns.

We have already discussed the tendency for marginal land, presumably pasture, to be given to the monasteries as granges between the eleventh and thirteenth century. Many of the place names for these pieces of land were familiar but some were completely unknown to me. For example, a land grant dated to between 1157 and 1170 describes a piece of land as, '...all Hornhouwald, namely from the land of Matthew and the bounds of Thoralby to the bounds of Sledmere and Towthorpe'. This short phrase tells us a great deal about the changing perception and use of the landscape at this time. Clearly the townships of Sledmere, Thoralby and Towthorpe were in existence and their boundaries were known and fixed. However there was an area of land that lay between the territories, which had its own name, *Hornhouwald*. This name has not survived in any form into the later documents. It has been lost but must originally have been used to describe this piece of marginal waste or pasture. The name *Hornhouwald* is interesting as it contains the *wald* element but also the Old Scandinavian element *haugr*, commonly found in place names as *how* or *hou*. The place name Huggate is made up of the *haugr* element and the Old Scandinavian word *gata* meaning 'road'. Place-name scholars have always translated this name as 'road to the mounds' or 'barrows' as barrow is the most common meaning of *haugr*. However, in some cases *haugr* can also be used to refer to hills.

The best-known examples of names with *haugr* are those like Duggleby Howe or Willy Howe which are actually names given to specific barrows. As I searched through the land charters there were more examples of these names using the *haugr* element and sometimes combining it with *wald*. A twelfth-century charter refers to 'the territory of Middleton' and describes it as lying 'on Mardererhau'. Another grant talks about an area on the boundary between Middleton and Londesborough called *Lothenhaues*. According to E.H. Smith, both names combine *haugr* with the personal names Maynard and Lodinn. There are many others from across the Wolds but some of these have vanished since the twelfth century and were only recorded in these grants. Other names using *haugr* have survived because they were transferred to names for townships like Haywold (*Houwald*) or Burrow (*Burre hou*).

Huntow was mentioned in the previous chapter. Located on the high ground inland from Bridlington it appears to have been the name of an extensive pasture shared out between the townships of Buckton, Grindale and Speeton. It also gave its name to the early medieval administrative territory or hundred from this area known as *Huntow*. It has always been felt that hundreds whose names contained *haugr*, such as *Thorshowe*, had been named after a barrow used as a central trial place or meeting point. It is equally likely that these territories were named after tracts of marginal wold land that by the twelfth century were being gradually colonised by villages and townships. These names have survived by chance. When they were being used in the twelfth century to describe a piece of land they were archaic and old fashioned. They tell us more about the kind of landscape that existed here before the Norman Conquest than that of the twelfth century. After the thirteenth century, pieces of land were described using the names of the townships and this new nomenclature slowly replaced the old terms (*51*).

Names like *Hornhouwald* are echoes from another world. They are dim reminders of a landscape that had otherwise been forgotten. The names are enticing as they bring this landscape of pastures and trackways to life in the period before the eleventh century. They evoke a marginal territory, which was removed from the heartlands of settlement and agriculture. This is the kind of place that became known as a wold. Harold Fox thought the same about the Wolds of the Midlands and Chris Wickham argued that the name wold was probably more about the rights and perception of these landscapes than their vegetation cover or topography.

LANDSCAPES OF THE DEAD

It took about six months for all these threads of evidence to come together into a coherent story line. The trackways and pastures were all part of the pastoral open landscape before the Norman Conquest. Until the tenth or eleventh centuries the settlements seemed to have lain around the wold-edges whilst the interior of the Wolds was used as pasture. Large chunks of it were probably attached to individual estates based at centres around the edge of the Wolds. Some settlements must have existed on the Wolds but these would have been occasional bases for herders or hunting parties. It wasn't until the tenth or eleventh centuries when many settlements began to be formed and the villages tended to grow up around the meres. At this time the township boundaries were laid out along some of the existing tracks and within each territory the open fields were also designed and created. The large pastures were then slowly portioned out between the townships. Finally the remaining pieces of marginal land were given out to monasteries and abbeys between the eleventh and thirteenth centuries.

There were some archaeologists who argued that the Wolds was inhabited between the fifth and ninth centuries and that the Anglo-Saxon settlement sites were just waiting to be found. If my ideas were right then we had not found these sites because they were not there in any great numbers. An unpublished paper by the place name scholar Margaret Gelling supported this view. She thought that:

> a falling off of numbers of people living in the northern part of the wolds and an increase starting in the eighth century and continuing into the tenth century is consistent with the archaeological record to date at Wharram Percy and … fits the place-name record.

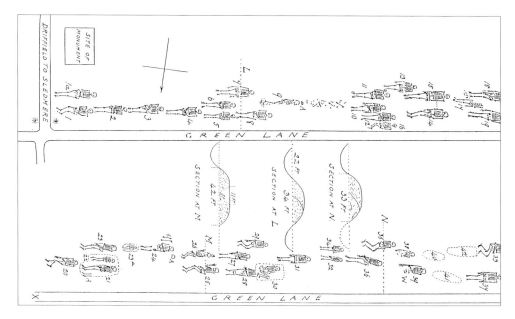

52 Mortimer's plan of excavated skeletons from the Anglo-Saxon cemetery along the linear ditch at Sykes Monument on the Sledmere Green Lane. *From Mortimer 1905*

The discoveries at Cottam of an Anglo-Saxon and Anglo-Scandinavian occupation site in the heart of the high Wolds made me re-evaluate this idea. What if there were more? Julian Richards, who excavated the site, believed that this discovery was to be the first of many similar sites of this date from the Wolds. However, at present this is only one of a few such settlements. It stands apart from many contemporary sites because of its high-status associations. There is every chance that an open pastoral landscape like this did contain the occasional occupation site. These could have been temporary settlements for hunting parties or shepherds. They were the kind of places that later on were used as the basis for the permanent settlements of the period after the tenth or eleventh century.

One other thread of evidence came along to add colour to the picture. I had become interested in the way that Anglo-Saxon society was obsessed with the past. There were many cases from across the country where prehistoric barrows were used as burial places for the Anglo-Saxon dead. Indeed this often happened in many occasions on the Wolds. Barrows like that at Uncleby and Driffield had been excavated by Mortimer and he had found tens of inhumations dug through the earthen mound that had originally been thrown up in the Bronze Age. There were linear cemeteries along the linear ditches at Sykes monument and Garton Gatehouse and there were many other secondary inhumations in barrows from across the Wolds (52). In fact there were very few Anglo-Saxon burials from the

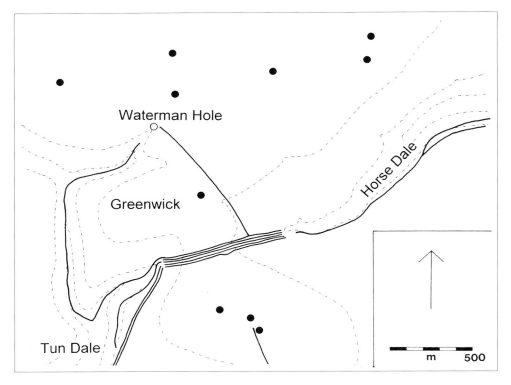

53 Part of the detached territory of Greenwick showing how it was enclosed by linear ditches. Huggate Dykes marked the southern boundary of this detached piece of Bishop Wilton township

Wolds that had not been inserted into much older mounds or banks. This was not the case at all around the wold-edge where most burials were part of flat inhumation cemeteries (*41*).

Andrew Reynolds had argued that secondary burials like these, in prehistoric barrows, were ways of disposing of the unwanted dead such as criminals or execution victims. Several of his examples were drawn from the Yorkshire Wolds but his ideas applied across the country. Sarah Semple has talked about how the Anglo-Saxons were afraid of the past. She showed that prehistoric burial mounds and relics dotted around the landscape were places shrouded in mystery and myths. The Wolds was covered in prehistoric burial mounds. If this landscape was remote from most settlements, it could easily have been seen as a fearful place partly because of the visible presence of the past. The only burials that were made here were those unwanted dead who could not be disposed of close to the home settlements. A plot of the Anglo-Saxon burials on the Wolds also shows that they were often situated close to trackways. This also supports the idea that the dead were deliberately placed away from home.

54 A view across the barren featureless arable landscape of the modern Wolds

This was a marginal landscape associated with the past but used for pasture. It was spread with strange earthen mounds whose name *haugr* may have been used in many of the place names coined to describe vast tracts of this landscape. Some of these names were matched with another word for the place, *wald*.

Thomas Hardy's image of Egdon Heath in *The Return of the Native* would not have been familiar to the medieval communities who lived on the Wolds but their ancestors who had used the vast tract for grazing in the eighth century AD would have known it. Egdon was littered with barrows and winding, wandering lanes crossed exposed terrain. It was the province of outcasts and itinerants. Outsiders lived here. The following extract comes from this book:

> Before him stretched the long, laborious road, dry, empty and white. It was quite open to the heath on each side, and bisected that vast dark surface like the parting-line on a head of black hair, diminishing and bending away on the furthest horizon.

SEVEN

ANOTHER TURN OF THE CYCLE: THE MEDIEVAL LANDSCAPE AND THE AGE OF ENCLOSURE

In this chapter, we shall consider the medieval and post-medieval landscapes of the Wolds. Great changes took place between the tenth and twelfth centuries. This involved the formation of the villages and open fields that characterised the medieval countryside as the open pasture of the Anglo-Saxon period was gradually colonised and farmed. This episode of settlement encroachment and increased land management can be compared with the changes we saw in the late Iron Age when this same landscape was divided, enclosed and farmed in a new and more intensive way. As part of this long-term history, the period between the tenth and twelfth century witnessed another turn of the cycle. As in the late Iron Age, the open pasture of trackways and burials was transformed into a countryside that was farmed and occupied. By the sixteenth century, things had moved on again. As the population declined and economic climate altered, many Wolds villages shrunk or were abandoned. Much of the Wolds landscape was turned into pasture again between the fifteenth and eighteenth centuries. Although these changes took place for very different reasons, the cycle kept on turning. The period of sheepwalks and rabbit warrens lasted until the eighteenth or nineteenth century when much of the Wolds was enclosed again and once more farmed in new intensive ways that had not been seen before.

We know a lot about the medieval landscape, mainly because there are many good documentary sources. There are records of field names, people, grants of land and the delimitation of estates. Court cases, deaths, wills and tax returns have all been recorded; even maps of the open fields survive. The most detailed historical sources for the open fields are maps which were drawn up at enclosure to document the strips and furlongs just as they were about to be enclosed with hedges. This was during the eighteenth and nineteenth centuries when the old collective system had declined and was being replaced by private enterprise and ownership.

The Wolds is well known for its many abandoned or shrunken medieval villages which have offered archaeologists a way of finding out about medieval settlement. The multi-disciplinary research at Wharram Percy has shown what can be done. Research has focussed largely on the villages but there has been very little attempt to reconstruct the layout and development of the open fields on the ground. Even though the earthwork remains of these fields have been ploughed, they are clearly visible from the air and the ridge and furrow earthworks can still be seen as curving stripes in the bare winter soil or the ripening crops.

VILLAGES AND OPEN FIELDS

The pattern of nucleated village surrounded by the open expanse of unhedged arable field was common throughout many parts of England, stretching from the south coast to the Pennines. During the eighteenth and nineteenth centuries, these same areas were enclosed by Act of Parliament creating the distinctive look of these landscapes today. The differences between the champion (open field) and woodland countryside have been recognised for many years and this distinction is still visible on the ground today. The landscapes of wooded hedges flanking winding sunken lanes with small, irregular fields and scattered hamlets are characteristic of ancient or woodland countryside like Essex, Devon and Somerset. The wide-open rectangular fields, broad-verged roads, nucleated villages and scattered enclosure farmhouses are what we see in champion countryside such as East Yorkshire or Cambridgeshire. These regional differences have their roots prior to enclosure. Even during the medieval period, there were distinctive regional landscapes and these deep rooted differences have never been properly explained.

The classic medieval open field system was a collective farming enterprise, which depended on cooperation between the members of each village community. We know how this worked from the documentary sources that have survived from the thirteenth century and later. Each householder held a number of shares in the land, known as *oxgangs* which represented rights to cultivate certain strips in the open field. The strips were spread evenly throughout the fields of the village territory or 'township'. At any one time, one of the great open fields would be left fallow, partly to allow the land to recuperate but mainly to provide grazing land for the livestock of the village. The animals were owned

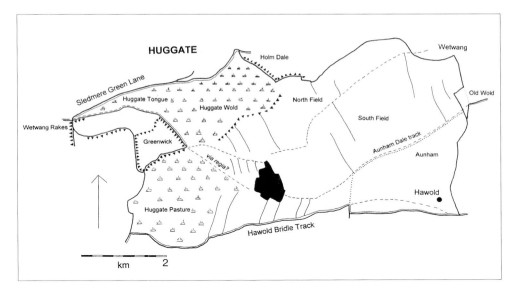

55 A reconstruction of the township of Huggate from eighteenth- and nineteenth-century sources. The pastures are present to the west of the territory. Hawold township occupied the south-east corner and was bounded on the north and west by the track along Aunham Dale. South Field and North Field denote the probable location of the open fields

separately by households but were grazed on common pastures. The open fields often stretched right across the township and left little space for permanent dedicated pasture. A manorial court regulated the activities of the farming year and this body made sure that each householder played by the rules. There was usually a right of pasture attached to each strip of arable and this dictated how many animals could be grazed in certain places at specified times of the year. These rights of pasture applied to both open fields in fallow, the stubble after harvest and the dedicated pasture grounds.

As already mentioned, some devoted pasture did exist on the more marginal tracts of wold land but these were the exception rather than the rule. Huggate was one example where much of the land was used for grazing all the time. In 1773, the 6000 acres of this township, which by this time included Haywold, were enclosed by Act of Parliament (55). The enclosure plan has not survived but the associated bill provides information about the organisation of livestock farming. There were three dedicated pastures called Oxpasture, Cowpasture and Huggate Tongue. Huggate Tongue was marked on the first edition OS map and was located in the northwest of the township, close to Wetwang Rakes and Greenwick (49 and 56). The other two pastures have not been located but Cowpasture Lane leads from Fridaythorpe towards the northern boundary of the township.

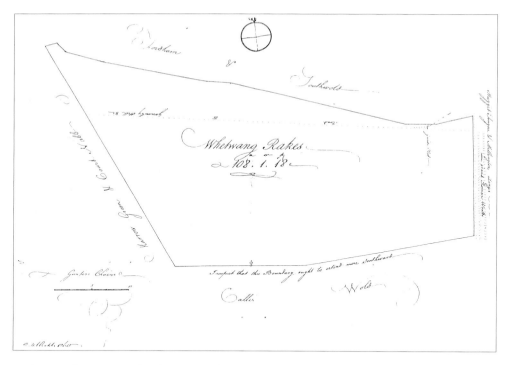

56 A map of Wetwang Rakes from 1760. This piece of detached pasture was intercommoned between Wetwang and Bishop Wilton. Along the eastern boundary is written: 'Huggit Tongue and Millington Ling and some grand Roman works' (DDCV179/22). *Courtesy of the Brynmor Jones Library, University of Hull*

The enclosure bill records a complex set of rules that governed grazing in these areas. In Huggate Tongue, for instance, the holders of ox gangs held grazing rights for sheep only. The sheep could only be grazed between Lady Day and Michaelmas, according to the old calendar. This must have been an archaic right, which had been in existence for many years. It is perhaps no accident that this particular pasture lay adjacent to Wetwang Rakes and Greenwick, which both appear to have been used as controlled grazing land for many centuries (*49*). There were only two arable fields in Huggate and one of these was always in fallow. During the winter, between October and April, the holders of strips in the field were allowed to graze their sheep in this fallow field. After April, the cottagers and commoners could also let their sheep into the field. Many more rights of way have survived in this township than in the adjacent territories and this could be related to the importance of livestock in the medieval and post-medieval periods. The paths would have been needed to move the animals around between pasture and shelter. They are likely to have survived for longer where they passed through grazing land than where they crossed cultivated ground.

57 Aerial photograph of Huggate village showing the earthworks and soil marks of deserted houses and plots from the medieval and post-medieval period. *Courtesy of Humber Archaeology Partnership*

The strips of the open fields were usually bundled into groups or furlongs and these came together to make up the wider field. In the Midlands, the strips in neighbouring furlongs lay in different directions to one another. However in East Yorkshire, the strips within one field tended to follow the same orientation and this has led to suggestions that they were laid out according to a single plan.

We touched on the question of the origins of the open fields and villages in the last chapter. This question has still not been fully resolved for any of the regions of England where open fields and nucleated villages were known. The earliest open field may have been in place by the ninth century, but they are not older than this. There are many examples where Anglo-Saxon settlements are known to be earlier than the open field and in these cases, the open fields must have been founded after the occupation sites were abandoned in the seventh to ninth centuries. By the thirteenth century, the open field system was well and truly in operation, complete with all the complex rules and regulations that governed it. Many medieval villages have survived to this day but were larger and more populous in medieval times. A large number have been abandoned. The earthworks of abandoned plots and houses can still be seen around the edge of villages like Huggate, Garton and Fimber (57). While the same villages existed, it would be wrong to think that this medieval landscape was a familiar one. The modern layout of hedged fields and wide roads was a product of the eighteenth and nineteenth centuries. In the Middle Ages, extensive arable fields, whose unhedged strips were interspersed with broad grassy balks and tracks, surrounded the villages (58). Each township contained between two and five of these fields and in some cases, they stretched from one township boundary to another. Quite apart from the lack of hedges or fences, a major difference to today would have been the greater number of people regularly working in the fields.

There is little doubt that the foundation of villages and the origins of open fields went hand in hand. However, it is unclear how radical this change was. Was it a drastic alteration as a new agrarian order was imposed or was it a much more gradual process? Some landscape historians have argued that the process was gradual as land was slowly taken into cultivation whilst at the same time isolated hamlets were transformed into nucleated settlements at the centre of the new fields. What looks like a planned system by the thirteenth century may actually have evolved slowly, beginning in the ninth or tenth centuries. In East Yorkshire, there is good evidence that many villages were deliberately planned. Some research suggests that even the open fields were laid out according to a single design. If both villages and fields were planned in this way, it would suggest a radical act of landscape design. But did it actually take place and if so, when?

58 A typical enclosure period road that followed the balk within the south field of Wetwang village

Historical geographers have studied the plans of medieval villages for decades. They search for the earliest evidence of the village layout and try to analyse the distribution of house plots, garths, roads, tofts and crofts. In many cases these layouts are very regular with equal and adjacent enclosures laid out along an axial street. At Wharram Percy, the ordered layout of tofts and crofts looks as if it was designed as a single plan but despite many years of work, it is still unclear exactly when this took place. Some nearby villages such as Wharram le Street were planned in the twelfth century but at Wharram Percy, it is possible the plan was made and executed before the Norman Conquest. The open fields that surround the village could also have been founded in the ninth or tenth centuries. Sheppard's work on documentary records of the 'fiscal carucates' from Domesday Book supports this. It suggests that much of the Wolds was already intensively cultivated by the eleventh century, when the Domesday survey was undertaken.

Mary Harvey has also looked at the origins of the open fields of East Yorkshire. She has used later map sources but related them to the earlier documentary records to try and identify the earliest arrangements of strips and furlongs in the fields. Her findings show that many townships on the Wolds have always had very long strips, sometimes stretching for over 1000m. The organisation of the furlongs and the way the strips are allocated to individual farmers all suggests that these fields were laid out according to a single township-wide design. The fields and villages within each township were probably laid out quickly and simultaneously. As June Sheppard points out, enclosure was a radical landscape change but spread over 150 years. If these changes began before the Norman Conquest, they may have originated in the landholding reorganisation that took place alongside the Scandinavian political takeover in the ninth and tenth centuries.

By the thirteenth century, this landscape had been transformed. The high chalky wastes, the steep dry valleys and the rolling grassland of the dip slope were now part of a patchwork of thriving agricultural communities. An earlier landscape dominated by pasture with occasional small-scale settlements was turned into well-managed and ordered farmland with an overwhelmingly arable basis. The places of antiquity that had previously been remote windswept spots, only occasionally visited for special meetings or festivals, were brought in to the everyday world. The ancient linear banks and ditches that had been followed by shepherds and travellers in the eighth century now ran along the edges of the open field. The ancient linear earthwork that is followed by the Sledmere Green Lane was used not only as the headland of the open field but also as the township boundary. The triple-ditch earthwork that passed Fimber village was also used as the edge of the arable field and the farmers would surely have marvelled at these banks and ditches as they went about their daily tasks. In some places where the ploughing encroached on the old ditches and barrows, human skeletons, flints and pottery would have been unearthed. Many barrows would have been ploughed up into the arable whilst others were fortuitously preserved in pastures located on the margins of the township areas. The trackways we talked about in the last chapter formed the boundaries of many of these townships and they continued to provide access still between communities on either side of the Wolds. The travellers would have known these roads were old for they had been there as long as anyone could remember. In chapter six, we saw how the Wolds landscape differed from the surrounding lowlands during the post Roman period before the Norman Conquest. However, by the thirteenth century, both wold and lowland vale shared many similarities. They were both farmed and occupied by villages and open fields and, whilst some differences may still have been recognised, these must have been less obvious than before the eleventh century or indeed after the sixteenth century.

DESERTED MEDIEVAL VILLAGES

In 1955, the *Yorkshire Archaeological Journal* ran an article that listed the sites of all the lost villages in Yorkshire. This was the beginning of an enquiry that revolutionised both landscape studies and medieval archaeology. By combining archaeological fieldwork with documentary research and addressing their investigations on a landscape scale, Beresford and Hurst spearheaded the multi-disciplinary ethic that now underpins all archaeological and historical work. The villages that Beresford listed were known from documentary sources but had disappeared from the map. His first intention was to find out why these settlements had been abandoned and the excavations at Wharram were one of the ways to do this. The desertion of lost villages was attributed to a number of economic or cultural forces such as the Black Death of 1349 or the economic decline of the fourteenth century. However, these were only two factors among many that affected settlement between the fourteenth and eighteenth centuries. At Wharram Percy, the village was deserted in the sixteenth century when four families were evicted from the site so that it could be turned over to sheep pasture. The village had already been in decline before this date and no single cause can be blamed for the depopulations. Another prime cause of village desertion came much later in the eighteenth century. At this time, landowners often moved villages to a new location so that their country houses could enjoy a more genteel pastoral landscape setting. Many stately homes and landscape parks were laid out in the late seventeenth and eighteenth centuries. Sledmere

59 Sledmere House and gardens

was a classic example: here the old village was depopulated and moved between 1750 and 1780. In the nineteenth century, a new estate village was built nearby, leaving the church isolated in the grounds (*59*). The majority of villages did not become abandoned overnight but were gradually de-populated. In some cases, there were still one or two householders left living at sites like Cowlam, Cottam, Eastburn or Towthorpe in the late seventeenth century. The hearth tax returns for 1672 show that many wolds villages, later to be deserted, still had a number of households and Susan Neave has shown that this was a gradual process caused by the ailing economic fortunes of the area (*61*).

The lost village of *Holm Archiepiscopi* is not mentioned in Domesday Book. The lands here belonged to the Archbishop of York but he granted them to Hexham Abbey in the eleventh century. In the thirteenth century, another Archbishop reacquired lands in the township. In 1381, the village returned 11 poll tax payers and probably contained a manor house and a chapel. By the seventeenth century, the records suggest that the village had become part of Wetwang parish (*60*). A document from the early seventeenth century records that:

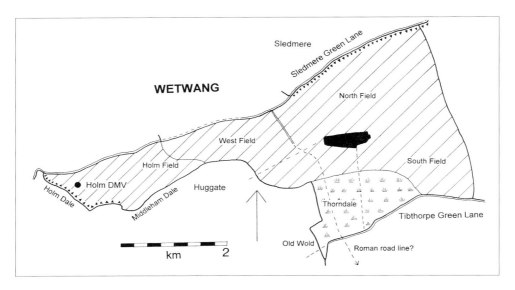

60 The township of Wetwang at enclosure in 1806. The pasture of Thorndale and the layout of its three open fields are shown. Holm Field was added during the seventeenth century once Holm village had been depopulated. The boundaries were marked by green lanes

> The prebend of Holme Archiepiscopus is Lord of the whole towne of Holme Archieopiscopie and hath all manner of temporall and spiritual jurisdiction of all the towne of Holme ... there is noe church there (that is to say) the inhabitants there are of the parish of Wetwang.

At enclosure there were four fields in Wetwang township and one of these was called Holm Field, located on the western edge of the territory around the site of the deserted settlement. This field must have been combined with the other fields after 1608 when Wetwang is known to have had only three fields. There are two field names recorded in the land grants of the twelfth century, which may also refer to this lost village. *Kikholmnab* and *Greneholm* can both be located on the boundary between Wetwang and Huggate in the vicinity of the site of Holm village. They probably refer to pieces of land granted to the church in *Holm* township.

PARLIAMENTARY ENCLOSURE

By the early eighteenth century, the English landscape was rapidly changing. A revolution in agricultural techniques led to radical changes to land ownership and management. All over the country, farmland was being 'improved' so that

61 The deserted medieval village of Cottam showing earthworks of former tofts and crofts. The church has been left isolated amongst the remains, which are now occupied by a classic enclosure period farmhouse. *Courtesy of Humber Archaeology Partnership*

private enterprise could turn a profit from the land. The self-sufficient agrarian system of open fields and common grazing gradually disappeared from most areas as small pieces of the open fields were enclosed and taken into private hands. However, on the Wolds the open fields survived. Village populations were in decline according to the collective practices that were centuries old but those that remained continued to farm. The agricultural improvers saw the potential in the land but realised they would have their work cut out if they were to overturn a system that was engrained in the people and their landscape. Writing in 1769, Arthur Young noted that the land on the Wolds was cultivated 'in a very indifferent manner'. Isaac Leatham, a land surveyor and enclosure commissioner, was contracted to produce a survey of the agricultural potential of the East Riding. Writing in 1794, he pointed out many instances where improvements could be made:

> The greater part of the Wolds townships which remain open, have a large quantity of out field in ley land, that is land which they take a crop of corn every third, fourth, fifth or sixth year, according to the custom of the township; after which they leave it without giving any manure or fallow ... the fold conducted in this manner is beneficial to the arable land, but the farmer does not consider how much he robs his pasture land...

Above: 62 The roads laid out at enclosure were straight and level with broad verges, flanked by short hawthorn hedges

Left: 63 A length of hawthorn hedge that must have followed the sinuous course of the strips in the open field

Between 1750 and 1850, virtually all the Wolds townships were enclosed by Act of Parliament. The landscape was changed utterly in the space of a century. Strickland, writing in 1812, glorified the transformations:

> The taste for inclosing has been carried out with great avidity in the East Riding and more acts of parliament have been obtained for that purpose during the last thirty years than at any former period. Indeed, very few unenclosed townships now remain in it.

In other parts of the country voices were raised against this process. The poems of John Clare lamented the loss of his beloved countryside but also criticised the affect these changes had on the lives of everyday people. Long-held common rights to land and grazing were lost overnight and many people must have been forced to move away from the villages or seek work in the mills and factories of the towns and cities. Their story in East Yorkshire remains largely untold for the historical records of their plight have not survived. Leatham was aware of the criticisms when he wrote, '... some are of the opinion that inclosures have been the cause of a decrease in population...'. But for him the benefits far outweighed the human cost:

> Additional labour, an improved air, and an increase in produce are certainly favourable to an increase in population, these are in general the beneficial consequences of inclosures.

Wetwang township was enclosed between 1803 and 1806. The accounts of the landowner, Lord Bathurst, for the decades leading up to enclosure have survived and they tell us a lot about improvements that were made (56 and 60). Lord Bathurst had commissioned his agent to assess the potential of the land at Wetwang for enclosure. He may have overstated the barren nature of this landscape to justify the need for radical change:

> The country is open, scarce a bush or tree appears for several miles. The land is stony and seems to be principally adapted for an improvement by St Foyn though the lower lands may bear clover and other seeds.

The agent consistently urged the landlord to increase the productivity of the land and by doing so to override the hereditary common rights of the villagers. At one point, he refers to the pasture on the southern edge of the township at Thorndale where tenants held rights to collect gorse for fuel and to graze their animals. For a long time they had leased these rights to other members of the township. Lord Bathurst's agent noted that:

64 Dew ponds like this one were constructed all over the Wolds during the eighteenth and nineteenth centuries to provide water for livestock away from the meres of the village

> The long custom of the tenants letting this land to the Town has misled them (the town) into an opinion that they have a right to it upon the terms now taken.

The Acts of Parliament gave the enclosure commissioners a free hand to completely redesign the landscape (*62* and *63*). The open fields were enclosed into a patchwork of neat rectangular fields, each one surrounded by short hawthorn hedges. New brick and pantile farmsteads were built out in the spaces between villages so that they were close to their land. Plantations of beech trees often surrounded these dwellings to shelter them from wind and break up the panorama. Roads were often laid out afresh and the winding course of old sunken ways was utterly obliterated. The old tracks had run along the dry valleys but the new straight and wide roads adopted direct routes across the wold tops. The characteristic landscape of the Wolds today was created under this scheme in the decades between 1750 and 1850.

EIGHT

RHYTHMIC CYCLES OF LIFE AND LANDSCAPE

There are places where memory resides. Where the past echoes loudly. They are held in stories, songs and journeys and they survive.

SPECIAL PLACES

My brother Kim has a different take on archaeology to mine. We have spent many days tramping about the Wolds searching out mysterious places. Faced with a barrow or boundary bank, we have both tried to explain the monument, to discover the thinking behind it and the meaning it once held. Kim tends to explain his world through mysteries and energies whilst my interpretations are less intuitive. Many times we have come across a place with a feeling; somewhere that feels different and special. This can rarely be explained, for the feelings are subtle and opaque and they cannot be measured. For example, climbing Glastonbury Tor fills me with wonder and excitement. I am unsure if this is because of the amazing view at the top, the strangeness of the terraces that surround the hill, the glory of the Somerset countryside or simply the knowledge that this place has held mysteries for people for so many centuries? In Durham Cathedral, I feel a sense of the serenity and faith, even though I am not a Christian. The centuries of devoted awestruck visitors can still be felt as a tangible force. The size, complexity and beauty of the architecture are marvellous but the sense of age and history prevails. It would not feel the same if this building had been constructed last year. A new shopping centre does not have this spirit but an old Victorian steelworks does. I feel the same when I wander up and down the massive earthen banks of Huggate Dykes, stand on top of Duggleby Howe or walk the approach to Fimber with its church atop a barrow sitting by a pond. These are relics of another world when this landscape meant something different to its inhabitants and visitors. These places survive in our memories and consciousness because they are relics from the past. Maybe, these places possess an energy, but it feels more like shadows from history or memories hanging in the air.

Prehistoric people knew the importance of places and the way that certain spots were favoured by their topography and aspect. This may originate in the primal instinct of hunters to be able to survey whole tracts of landscape but there is no doubt that from the very earliest times in human history we have responded to special places. Monuments from all periods of prehistory are often gathered together in the same place, even though centuries of time and generations of life separate them. Stonehenge is one dramatic example of a place which was sacred for many centuries with successive generations adding their own contemporary twist to the architecture of the monument and its surroundings.

So far in this book we have traced the history of this landscape period by period, travelling steadily through time from the past to the present. In doing so, we can sometimes miss the wonder of the long-term survival of certain places and how they were repeatedly respected and used by communities over many centuries. In this chapter, we will consider the long-term survival of certain places and then discuss the long-term history of the landscape as a whole.

CRAIKE HILL

Craike Hill is located a few miles west of Driffield. It is unremarkable as all of the many mounds, banks and barrows have been ploughed into the arable fields. To visit, take the Ordnance Survey 1:25,000 map (Explorer sheet 294) and go to the village of Garton on the Wolds, a few miles west of Driffield. Park the car on the east side of the village and walk down the lane called Garton Balk heading south towards Kirkburn. This was formerly the edge of the open field and marked the boundary between the townships of Garton and Elmswell. The field boundaries on your left are fossilised remains of strips from the open field whilst those on your right were newly laid out at Enclosure in 1774.

After about a kilometre, you will come across another track heading off at right angles to the right. This is the corner of tracks visible on the right-hand

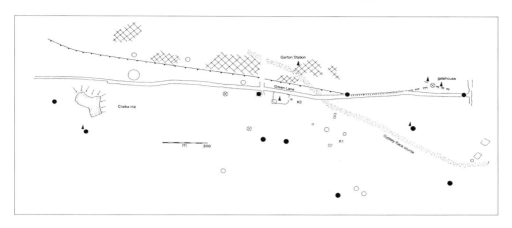

65 The concentration of burial monuments at Craike Hill and Garton Station. The Tibthorpe Green Lane runs across the centre of the picture. A linear earthwork following an earlier track is marked by hachures. Groups of Anglo-Saxon burials are marked by triangles; Iron Age cemeteries as hatched zones; Bronze Age and Neolithic barrows are marked as circles, those in solid black were relict in the nineteenth century whilst the other barrows are cropmarks. *Information from Stead 1991, Mortimer 1905, Stoertz 1997, Dent 1983*

side of the map featured in fig. 65. Take this lane for it marks the Green Lane that heads westwards from this point for several miles. The lane once continued to the east but this has been lost over the last 200 years. It probably carried on to the south-east heading across the old airfield. As you walk westwards along the Green Lane you have the lowlands of the upper Hull Valley behind you and the beginning of the Wolds in front. The low rolling landscape is characteristic of the eastern dip slope and it is here that Wetwang-Garton Slack opens out and the chalk and gravels give way to clays.

The whole area on either side of this lane was dotted with barrows, linear earthworks and other more obscure prehistoric monuments. These relics were grouped around the junction of two ancient trackways. One more or less followed the Green Lane in a westerly direction, which gradually climbs up on to the chalk. The other took a sweeping curve along the floor of the great valley towards the north-west. This track is known from aerial photographs and was excavated in places such as Wetwang Slack further up the valley. The two tracks came together at Craike. This place and these trackways have been sacred since about 3000 BC as there were late Neolithic barrows and enclosures here. The Neolithic monuments marked the place for the first time. An occupation site was discovered on Craike Hill to the west, a low natural hill that has been used over recent decades as a quarry.

A thousand years later, many Bronze Age barrows were constructed here and they must have been placed deliberately close to the existing and visible Neolithic monuments. The old course of the (Driffield) Gypsey Race runs through the centre of the monument complex and this would have added to the significance of this place for prehistoric communities in a landscape that possessed very few surface supplies of running water.

Two thousand years after the round barrows, during the Iron Age, many square barrow burials were concentrated in this small area alongside the track at the beginning of the Wolds. Two large cemeteries are known from aerial photographs and Ian Stead has excavated several of the barrow cemeteries. He found some unique and special graves. The deceased in one of the cart burials had been given a coat of chain mail, lain over the corpse in the grave. Other burials appeared to have been ritually speared once they had been placed in the grave. During the Iron Age, this may have been a place for the unusual or unwanted dead to reside. The shepherds and travellers that passed by these barrows on their way into the chalky pastures would have hurried past these sites, remembering half forgotten stories of the funerals and ceremonies that had taken place.

We cannot be sure how this place was used or viewed during the Roman period for there is no archaeological evidence from that time. That does not mean that people did not use it for meetings or festivals but we do not see the place used again for burial and monuments until the Anglo-Saxon period. This was a time, like the middle Iron Age period of square barrows, when the Wolds to the west was a place of remote open pasture. Most of the Anglo-Saxon burials were probably placed here around the seventh or eighth centuries. There were two cemeteries whose graves were dug along the base of a linear earthwork ditch. Several other inhumation graves were deliberately made in enclosures and barrows of Iron Age date. Further groups of inhumations were inserted into Bronze Age round barrows between this place and Driffield, 3km to the east. For the Anglo-Saxon community, this must have been a very important spot. Both trackways were almost certainly in use at this time but the burials were placed here because of the many visible and varied ancient monuments that were gathered here.

The Green Lane trackway that bisected the site was then adopted as a township boundary probably between the ninth and eleventh centuries. The place was used as the meeting place for the whole East Riding. In the thirteenth century, the Riding court was described as 'thrithingum de Crakou' (Craike) and another reference from the end of that century refers to it as 'trithing de Gartem' (Garton). We do not know how far back this role extended but this location must have already been used for gatherings, councils and perhaps trials for many centuries. The moots or meeting places of early medieval wapentakes or hundreds were often located in just this sort of marginal mysterious place and were regularly associated with ancient mounds, barrows or crosses.

66 Looking south towards the roundabout east of Fimber village. This was the spot where several linear earthworks and trackways came together where the valleys join

Places such as this were important to many successive generations of people who were well aware of the relics of the past that could be seen. The stories and names given to them are lost to us now and there is no trace of the gatherings and festivals that must have occurred. These places were used to make some sense of the past and to firmly root these communities in their landscape and ancestral line. They are places of memory and places of myth. It is hard to imagine what this place once looked like but we can at least refer to the cropmark plot or even the Ordnance Survey 6in map to witness the distribution of barrows.

It is harder though to imagine how people felt about these ancient relics dotted together alongside the path. One thing that is certain is that the meanings of this place survived in the memories of local people for thousands of years. The sense of the past was kept alive through the names given to the barrows, the stories that were told about these strange mounds and the myths about their origins. It was at places like this where the history of these communities resided and where this sense of a mysterious mythical past was brought to life.

FIMBER

Another aged place is the area around Fimber village. From Wetwang take the main road towards Malton, the B1248. This road takes you along the western end of Wetwang Slack, the opposite end of the valley to Craike Hill. At Fimber, the valley bottom is narrower and the sides are steeper than they are around Garton and Craike (*66* and *67*).

Before the roundabout at Fimber Nab, there is a picnic spot and car park on the left-hand side of the road. Park here on the site of the old railway station and study your map to take stock of where you are in relation to the surrounding landscape. Because of the railway line, this place was easily accessible in the nineteenth century and many interested antiquarians came here to marvel at the banks and ditches that converged on the village (*19*). Mortimer himself was brought up in the village and he wrote two detailed articles on its prehistory in the late nineteenth century. Thomas Wiltshire wrote in 1861:

> Towards the north-western side of the hilly district, known by the name of the 'Wolds' and cut through by the old coach road from York to Bridlington are the remains of an ancient entrenchment which once completely encircled, though at some distance, the small village of Fimber.

At this time, the best-preserved stretches of earthwork could be found in an old plantation near the railway station. This field has now been ploughed and any traces of the once massive banks and ditches have been levelled, although they are still visible as cropmarks from the air. The roundabout is located at the junction of two dry valleys (*17*). One is known as Broad Dale and heads north-east towards Sledmere. The other is Burdale or Bessingdale and sweeps from here towards Thixendale village.

To the north and west of this point, there are the classic Wolds landscapes of dry valleys winding through the domed chalk plateaux. To the south and east the countryside is more undulating and in this direction, the land gradually flattens out to the dip slope and the lowlands of Holderness. The two valleys become narrower and steeper as they progress to the north and west and the point where they come together has been marked repeatedly by the people who occupied this landscape over the last 2000 years.

The importance of the junction of valleys is best shown in the pattern of linear earthworks, which as we saw in chapter two, tend to follow the lay of the land. The builders of these boundaries were using them to fix an idea in the landscape. They followed trackways and valleys and mimicked the shape of the dales with their V-shape profile. All the valleys that run down to this spot from Sledmere

67 Looking north-west, showing the curving course of the ditch running down Bessingdale towards the Fimber roundabout. The junction of valleys can be seen in the middle distance. *Courtesy Humber Archaeology Partnership*

and the north-east were followed by linear earthworks and here, where they converge, they were provided with a multiple row of banks and ditches as a way of emphasising the point.

These massive banks and ditches were those that both Mortimer and Wiltshire marvelled at in the 'old plantation' (*19*). They ran across the spur of land to the north of the roundabout, connecting one tributary valley with another. As Wiltshire noted, one of the old coach roads to Bridlington ran along these earthworks. This stretch of road was moved down to its present location around the time the railway was built in the mid nineteenth century. The layout of the linear banks and ditches is well recorded on the 1854 OS map and it is clear that the township boundaries have followed the line of these banks. Not only does the boundary run along the line of the earthworks but also, it then turns back on itself, creating a strange peninsula, only 10m in width between two parallel boundaries. What is more, the boundary sticks closely to the linears both to the north and south. This had been a crossroads for many centuries before the linears were even built. Like Craike, it was where two natural routeways converged and as such it was a place where people came together. Monuments built here would have been seen by many passing travellers.

The village of Fimber is another place to which people came back again and again over the centuries (*colour plate 30*). It lies on a broad natural shelf that looks like it might have been hewn out of the valley side. In the centre of the village were two ponds. There is only one left but both were recorded in the nineteenth century. They were almost certainly natural meres and sat on pockets of clay, which has retained rainwater for many centuries (*17*). These ponds were the only source of water for the villagers until the nineteenth century when a well was dug. Until then one was used for the animals and the other for humans. Like Sledmere, the village of Fimber was named after its mere and the fact that this word has Old English origins show that the mere must go back to at least the seventh century. The open landscape of the Wolds in prehistory and during the Anglo-Saxon centuries were predominantly places of pasture and this was one of the very few water sources that existed. Herders, traders and travellers would have come to this place but there is very little evidence of any permanent settlement until the medieval village. The name *Fin mere* was probably given to this place before it became a village, but it had clearly been a place of congregation for many centuries before.

The existing church stands proud above the few houses and was built in the nineteenth century by the Sledmere estate. You can see the similarities in architectural style between it and the memorial spire located by the Sledmere Green Lane and raised to Sir Tatton's memory. But this Victorian church replaced a ruined predecessor and, judging by the architectural details on photographs of the ruin, this must have been medieval in date. The significant thing about this church is that it sits on top of a Bronze Age barrow. Mortimer spent time excavating this barrow and found the remains of the original prehistoric interment as well as a number of Anglo-Saxon burials. Although his records are vague, he also discovered the burnt timber remains of another building which was earlier than the medieval church. He saw this as the first timber church but without any further information we cannot be sure of the date or the function of this building. The barrow was placed here to mark the spot by the meres and thereafter the burials were laid inside the barrow to reaffirm the importance of this place. The layout of the linear earthworks, probably dug in the late Bronze Age also focus attention on the ponds as the massive parallel banks and ditches surround the modern village.

Places like this were consistently and repeatedly significant to the Wolds communities over many centuries. They were important because of the topographic location and in this case the water sources, but also because they were places where the past was visible. During the Anglo-Saxon period in particular, people made sense of the past through engagements with relics such as this barrow. For agrarian societies, their whole notion of the past and their

68 The earthworks at Huggate Dykes, looking west. The surviving banks and ditches can be seen in the middle distance whilst their ploughed down remains appear as cropmarks in the field in the foreground. A single surviving ditch runs along the right hand side of this field flanking the access road to the earthworks beyond. The topographic situation of the dykes is clear as they emanate from the head of a steep dry valley. *Courtesy English Heritage Crown copyright*

own history was worked out through stories and myths, which were told about places like this. It is no surprise then that when the new belief systems such as Christianity took hold in the seventh and eighth centuries, the new Christian monuments were built at places that already held spiritual significance. Building a church on top of a barrow was not a means of destroying the pagan forces that resided there. It was more a way of absorbing the magical and powerful energies into a new faith. The same process took place at Rudston, where the church was built next to a massive single standing stone. Today, the stone still stands in the churchyard. In pre-Christian societies, people did not get their sense of history from books but from stories they were told and the landscape that surrounded them. Names related to mythology and the ancestors were given to special places and landscape features such as trees, mounds, valleys and hills.

HUGGATE DYKES

We have already mentioned the Huggate Dykes and they are an important part of this landscape story. The Reverend E. Maule Cole was vicar of Wetwang in the late nineteenth century and he explained in an article of 1888 that: 'It may

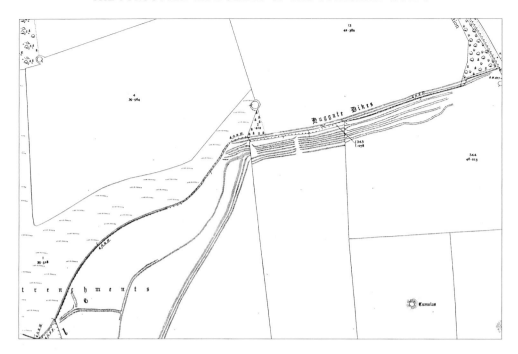

69 The linear earthworks at Huggate Dykes as they were in 1910. The banks in the field to the east have since been ploughed down but those in the two western fields have survived. *Ordnance Survey 1910 25in series*

be confidentially affirmed that they are, with the exception of the so-called Danes dike, the most remarkable entrenchments on the Wolds.' These banks and ditches have survived well because they were part of the glebe land under the jurisdiction of the Rector of Huggate. It is easy to visit this monument and a visit is essential to appreciate both the scale of the earthworks and to witness their setting in the landscape (*68* and *69*). The site lies to the west of Huggate village on the road towards Fridaythorpe and Thixendale. The monument has no signs or parking spaces but heading north-west from Huggate you can pull up on the left-hand side of the road just before Farclose Plantation. There is then a trackway that takes you away from the road to the monument.

Standing by the car you will be able to appreciate the location chosen for these banks. This is a short stretch of land between the heads of two dry valleys. Horse Dale runs off towards Sledmere and Wetwang to the north-east whilst the prodigiously steep slopes of Tun Dale descend towards the south-west and the wold-edges at Millington (*12*, *15*, and *16*). For travellers crossing the Wolds from any direction, this neck of land was crucial if you wanted to avoid traversing the steep slopes of any of the dry valleys. The modern road is probably following the

70 The Sykes monument erected to the memory of Sir Tatton Sykes built in 1865

line of a much older track, which gave its name to Huggate village, *haugr gata*, or 'road to the mounds'. At the spot where the car is parked, another trackway crossed this one and this is likely to be one of the earliest routes across the Wolds for it was followed by a massively long linear earthwork first constructed in the later Bronze Age.

One of the earliest maps of the Wolds produced in 1744 by Haynes marks the banks and ditches of Huggate Dikes. At this time, they ran across the full width of the natural bridge between the valleys, a distance of about 800m. Six banks and five ditches ran parallel across the water divide and they marked the importance of this piece of ground by providing the monument with multiple rows of banks and ditches. The earthworks have been gradually eroded and ploughed over the last 200 years and today are only preserved for a stretch of about 200m (*69*). The track, which takes you to the surviving banks, runs along the top of a single bank whilst its adjacent ditch can be seen clearly to the right. The rows of multiple earthworks are probably late Bronze Age in origin but there is little direct dating evidence. As we saw in chapter six, they form the southern boundary of a territory known as Greenwick, which is surrounded by single banks and ditches (*53*). These may be later additions made in the post Roman period to enclose a piece of pasture as the Wolds was being divided amongst the nascent villages and townships. Over 30 years ago, Varley excavated a section across the dikes and found an Anglo-Saxon cremation vessel, inserted into the one of the banks. This again shows how this place and this monument remained significant because of its topographic location and antiquity.

THE SLEDMERE GREEN LANE

In chapter six, we talked a lot about the Green Lane south of Sledmere that had once been a coach road but had its origin as a much more ancient trackway. This route tells the story of the Wolds countryside more than any other feature. The line in the landscape followed by a linear earthwork, township boundaries and then the eighteenth-century coach road was based ultimately on a prehistoric trackway (*colour plate 23*). This line was continually respected and used from at least 2000 BC to the present day, showing the amazing capacity for long term survival.

The line itself was repeatedly respected but it changed its function more than once, as it was used successively as either trackway or boundary. During those periods when the Wolds landscape was enclosed, divided and farmed, the Green Lane was a boundary. At those times when the landscape was open pasture it was a track. The history of this landscape goes through a process of cyclical change and the Green Lane mirrors this process (*72*). A walk along this lane takes you close to the history of the Wolds itself.

The best place to start is the Sykes monument alongside the B1252 between Sledmere and Garton on the Wolds where there is a small car park (*71*). The setting of this monument is as striking as the spire is pretentious. It sits on the ridge that marks the northern edge of the Wetwang–Garton Slack and commands extensive views to the south and east towards Driffield, Beverley and Holderness. On clear days, there are uninterrupted views as far as the Humber. This location was chosen as a memorial for two reasons. From here, Sykes continued to cast his paternal eye over the land he had owned and 'improved' but it was also placed here so that the spire would be visible from far away. The man's memory has thus become rooted in this place forever. The building of the monument was a grand statement made by a self confident family who believed that their ownership of the land was as natural and god given as their aristocratic privilege. It is a relic from the past and demonstrates a way of thinking that has all but disappeared.

The Green Lane began as a prehistoric trackway probably used during the Neolithic and Bronze Age but it is very difficult to pin down its origins exactly (*22*). The route as a whole follows the topography very closely and this stretch between

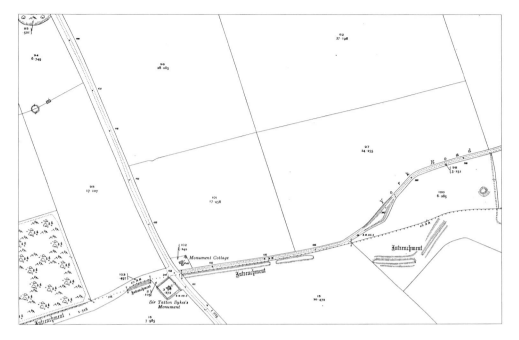

71 The area around Sykes monument showing the linear earthworks running from left to right along the course of the track. York Road marks the old coach road and to the south of that is the township boundary between Garton and Sledmere. The Sledmere Green Lane is the broad track to the west of the monument. *Ordnance Survey 1910 25 inch series*

the monument and Huggate Dykes to the west effectively links one group of dry valleys with another by sweeping broadly across the intervening land. In places, the prehistoric route was different to the line followed by the post Roman routeway and that in its turn is not exactly the same as the eighteenth-century coach road (*71* and *72*).

One of the places where they diverge is just to the east of the Sykes monument at the head of Warren Dale. If you walk eastwards from the car park, there is a narrow lane that follows the Green Lane. The massive bank of the linear earthwork is visible in the field to the right and it was here that the Granthams excavated the Anglo-Saxon cemetery in the 1950s.

The Green Lane began life as a trackway but was followed by linear banks and ditches during the late Bronze Age (*12*). These monuments still survived in the nineteenth century and can be seen on the first edition OS maps. They have been ploughed over the last 100 years and only survive in exceptional circumstances on the edge of fields or in woodland. There is a well preserved stretch of bank and ditch in Black Wood alongside the Green Lane to the west of the Sykes monument. From here you can walk along the Green Lane to the west.

The Green Lane was revered as an ancient monument with historic credentials that go way back to a distant past. As the communities here tried to change the meaning of the lane, they were drawing on this sense of history to bring more weight of tradition to their alterations. During the late Iron Age, the hillside to the south of the Green Lane was slowly being divided up and enclosed and occupied by small farmsteads (*27*). These are the slopes you are looking down over as you walk along the lane by High Bitings. Each occupation site was connected to a series of ditched boundaries that could have divided the land of one group from another. They also linked the land and dwellings of the different communities. The thing about these ditches is that they all ran up and down the valley side and led ultimately to the Green Lane earthwork banks. These banks would have been over 500 years old when this valley side was being enclosed around the first century BC. They were using the Green Lane as a reference point not only in space but also in time to which the new boundaries could be fixed.

Another example of the reuse of the past comes from the Anglo-Saxon period when an inhumation cemetery was inserted into the ditch of the earthwork up at the Sykes monument (*52*). The cemetery had been placed in the ditch of the earthwork and has been found on both sides of the road, similar to the other linear cemetery found at Craike Hill. This Anglo-Saxon burial sited along the southern boundary of Garton township, also followed a post Roman trackway across the Wolds. These burials were probably placed here at the same time as both these trackways were starting to be recognised and used as boundaries, sometime during the ninth century AD. By placing the dead of the community within the ditch, people were trying to change the way the banks and ditches were perceived (*47* and *48*). They drew on the power of the monuments as relics from the past to change the meaning they held in the present from trackway to boundary. The next alteration in the role of the Green Lane came during the eighteenth century when the track was used as a coach road (*42*).

CULTURAL REGIONS AND THE *PAYS*

In the centuries before the industrial revolution the landscapes of Britain were inhabited by agrarian societies, living in rural settings and rarely moving away from their places of birth. Long ancestral lines of local families were rooted to specific areas of the country and successive generations often farmed the same land in the same way for many centuries. This meant that the ties between people and the land were strong and that the cultural identity of communities was closely linked to the surrounding landscape.

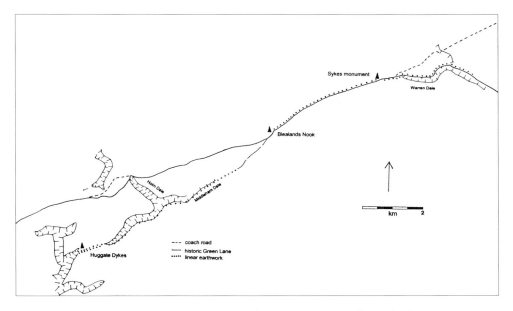

72 The many phases of the Sledmere Green Lane between Huggate Dykes and Sykes monument. The course of the continuous township boundary is marked by a solid line. The map shows how the earlier track followed by the linear earthwork ran to the south of the later post Roman track

The topographers who travelled around Britain between the seventeenth and nineteenth centuries took an interest in the changes taking place in farming practice and the differences that existed between regional landscapes. They often remarked upon the way that the differences in landscape character were also reflected in contrasts between the communities who inhabited these areas. For these post-medieval social geographers, Britain was divided naturally into regions. These did not always have clear or fixed boundaries but were part of the topography of the land. The Cotswolds, the Weald, the Yorkshire Moors, the South Downs are all topographic zones which in an agrarian society were also cultural areas whose communities tended to adopt similar forms of society and agriculture. Prior to the eighteenth century, the economic and cultural lives of the inhabitants of these areas differed from their neighbours as much as the landscape itself.

Archaeologists and historians do not always admit that they use literature as inspiration for imagining what life and landscapes were like in the past. Many were attracted to the subject by reading Tolkien, Susan Cooper or Mary Stewart. The search for the fantastic and the different is what drives their imaginations to creatively interpret the evidence from both the soil and the documents. The link between landscape and people is hard to quantify or describe. It can be seen in the writings of Thomas Hardy who was acutely aware of the character of landscape and used its melancholy and mystery to frame his tragic tales. As his characters wander from one area to another, he describes the changes in the landscape and people as the mood of the story is also transformed. For example, Hardy writes in *Tess of the D'Urbervilles*:

> Having already traversed about five miles on the upland she had now some ten or eleven in the lowland before her journey would be finished. The winding road downwards became just visible to her under the wan starlight as she followed it, and soon she paced a soil so contrasting with that above it that the difference was perceptible to the tread and the smell. It was the heavy clay land of Blackmoor Vale, and a part of the vale to which turn-pike roads had never penetrated. Superstitions linger longest on these heavy soils. Having once been forest, at this shadowy time it seemed to assert something of its old character....

Hardy was a close witness to the transformations in the nineteenth-century countryside and did not like what he saw. He was sensitive to the importance that landscape had in framing the lives of its inhabitants and setting them apart from their neighbours. The same idea is also present in *The Lord of the Rings* where places like the *Shire* and *Mordor* stand in stark contrast to one another both in the character of the landscape and the mood of the people.

We have seen how archaeology sets the Wolds apart from the surrounding lowlands and that its landscapes were occupied in different ways to the vales. While differences between regional landscapes must have been important to communities living before the Roman period, the nuance of these perceptions has been lost to us through the lack of written evidence. There may be hints from the evidence presented here that the Wolds did possess a different character to the surrounding lowlands. This was especially true during the middle Iron Age and Anglo-Saxon periods when the landscape was largely uninhabited and used mainly for pasture.

LONG-TERM LANDSCAPE HISTORY

Everyone who studies landscape history is still overshadowed by W.G. Hoskins, and his seminal work *The Making of the English Landscape*. This book presents a period-based history of the English countryside and even though some of his ideas are now out of date, it was recently revised. A spin-off from this book was the publication of a series of regional landscape histories produced in the 1960s and 1970s. They were based on the Hoskins formula and took the reader through each successive period of landscape change in England. Keith Allison wrote the volume for East Yorkshire, which was published in 1976. These regional landscape histories were an antidote to the traditional history of kings, queens and conquests or to the prehistoric equivalent of typologies of pots and daggers. They presented the history of everyday land and settlement and showed the reader how their local countryside had developed. We were encouraged to look about the place and investigate the landscape for ourselves.

I have tried to build on the insight and overview that Allison's study provided but would never suggest that this book is as wide in its coverage. In these pages we have specifically focused on the Wolds and have tried to bring to life a certain kind of lost landscape. I have tried to weave a coherent thread through the long-term sequence and this has involved not only making connections between periods but also recognising the long-term survival of many features in the landscape. The story of the Wolds landscape unfolds not as a sequence of disjointed separate periods but as a series of rhythmic cycles of transformation. The cycles were linked to one another but they were not the same. The survival of trackways and boundaries as lines in the landscape does not imply that this countryside never changed. The lines, such as the Green Lane, survived for many centuries but their meaning and function was constantly being altered. What is more, the people who were actively transforming these meanings were doing so by deliberately drawing on the idea of the track or boundary bank as a relic from the distant past.

The Hoskins school were historians first and foremost. Their writing does not do justice to the prehistoric period, which was often seen simply as a mysterious or environmental backdrop to the real story. They also tried to fit the history of the landscape into an historical period-based scheme. This was based on national cultural periods (Bronze Age, Iron Age), political changes (Roman occupation) or even the family lines of kings and queens (Tudor, Stuart). Traditional period divisions mean very little on the ground. Local communities belonged to their landscape and were slow to change when political alterations took place in other parts of the country. These communities inhabited a landscape that was full of the past and their identities were probably based on how these ancient places were woven into contemporary life. The trackway that the shepherds and flocks followed had been used for many centuries and it passed by the curious mounds from former times whose meaning had been lost. This was a place where you might fear to go at night in case the spirits that dwelt there escaped.

We have seen how the history of this landscape cannot be separated into neat period-based compartments and that folk memory survived for very long periods as certain special places were revered for thousands of years. When change occurred, it did not always coincide with the expected boundaries between periods. The massive period of enclosure, land division and settlement expansion in the first century BC came before the Roman Conquest. This had little obvious effect until the end of the second century. The beginning of the Bronze Age is defined by the first time that copper alloy was made, but this act did not change the lives or landscapes of the people of the Wolds. The first iron swords did not revolutionise lifestyles or farming methods and iron was probably still an expensive luxury by the time of the Roman Conquest. Communities living here during the Iron Age did not identify themselves by their common use of iron. This is the story of the way that the communities who lived here inhabited and worked with their landscapes. They used the landscape to express their relationship with nature, with each other and with their own ancestral past. Stories, names, songs and festivals were all woven into the valleys, meres, trackways and barrows to make sense of the past and to memorise this for the future.

When change does take place it happens on different levels. The annual cycle of seasons, sun and moon was probably the most potent calendar for these agrarian communities right up until the eighteenth century. Below this was the daily ritual from sunrise to sunset again governed by the sun and by work. Over and above, the agricultural cycles were longer-term cycles of lifetimes and family generations. Beyond this was memory and myth precariously preserved in stories, places and names. Since the eighteenth century, these perceptions of time have been replaced with a linear scheme using calendar dates and years. Time is now progressing onwards from a fixed point in the past towards another in the future. For this reason, we have come to assume that history works in this linear fashion. The landscape of prehistory became gradually more and more intensively farmed and inhabited as each successive generation of farmers built upon what had gone before. Population increased and technology advanced. The reality of long-term change in the landscape is much more complex but is rarely studied because archaeologists and historians tend to stick to specific periods. The long-term history is rarely seen as nobody steps back far enough to take it all in.

In periods such as the middle Iron Age or fifth to ninth centuries AD, the place was hardly inhabited but used instead for pasture by communities living around the wold-edges. Archaeologists have been looking for the settlements of the Iron Age and the Anglo-Saxon Wolds. They have often argued that these sites are simply waiting to be found. If these cycles are real, then their quest may never be successful for the settlements were simply not there in any great number. At times like this the landscape was uninhabited and crossed by long-distance trackways giving access to distant pastures, used on a seasonal basis. The open pastoral phases gave way dramatically to periods of enclosure and occupation.

The expansion of settlement and agricultural exploitation took place during the later Iron Age and just before the Norman Conquest when new settlements were founded and land was divided with boundaries. It happened again at enclosure when the sheepwalks, warrens and under-utilised open fields were partitioned and intensively farmed once more.

The periods of pasture and tracks were similar to one another but not exactly the same. The reasons for settlement demise and the return of the flocks was not the same in AD 500 as it was in AD 1600. Likewise the economic and social forces working behind the rise of enclosure and settlement expansion in 100 BC were not the same as those in operation in AD 900. Both the middle Iron Age and Anglo-Saxon periods saw the Wolds as a place of pasture remote from most settlements. At both times, the place was also used for burial but this worked in different ways for each period. In the Anglo-Saxon period, the burials were those of criminals and enemies and were placed here amidst the barrows of the past because they held fear and mystery. At this time, the Wolds landscape was a place to avoid, a world of malevolent spirits. During the Iron Age, I think the landscape of the dead was seen in another way. Carrying the dead of the community up into the chalk hills along well-worn paths was a way of returning the dead to an ancestral landscape, a heartland.

Many villages were abandoned on the Wolds during the post-medieval period and this led to large areas of the landscape reverting to pasture in what Fox calls the 'return of the flocks'. Between the seventeenth and nineteenth centuries, the Wolds was a remote place. Enclosure came and changed all that by laying out new fields and farms and applying new farming techniques to the land. Since the Second World War, these farming methods have become even more intensive and mechanised and fewer people are now needed to work on the land. The change from the extensive pastures of the seventeenth century to the intensive farming of today is not the culmination of a progressively more complex sequence but the turn of another cycle. The history of the Wolds landscape from as far back as 1000 BC has always worked like this. Harold Fox has recognised it in the post-Roman landscapes of the Wolds.

> The evidence for a good deal of woodland and open pasture on the Wolds, not to mention their use as seasonal grazing grounds, suggests that permanent settlements were relatively sparsely spread in the seventh and eight centuries AD, except in some favoured spots. At that time these regions were at a low point in one of those cycles of occupation followed by depopulation which they may well have witnessed before in prehistory, and which they were to witness once again in later centuries.

These cycles of transformation are visible on the Wolds much more clearly than on the surrounding lowlands. The plain of Holderness and the Vales of York and Pickering did not go through a similar interrupted history. They do not have phases of unmanaged wilderness interspersed with periods of intensive farming and occupation. There was something about the Wolds that always set them apart from their surroundings. But what was it? Some would say the answer must lie in the distinctive soils or topography of the place. I would prefer a cultural explanation and I believe the answer may lie in the rights of landholding. We have seen how the villa estates of the third century AD were attracted to the Wolds as a place where it was easier to manage and exploit large areas of agricultural land. This may be because the rights to that land held by its inhabitants during the second century were not very strong. Admittedly, some of these settlements had been in place for 200 years but we do not know what kind of land tenure bound the communities to the land they occupied. These rights may not have been as fixed as those found on the wold-edges and the vales where occupation had been much more long lived.

In chapter five, we discussed the meaning of the word *wald*. The traditional view is that the Old English word refers to 'woodland' but that this meaning then changed to describe 'open high ground'. Fox has argued that the post-Roman Wolds were areas of wood pasture with frequent stands of trees intermingled with areas of open ground. For the Yorkshire Wolds, there are very few references to woodland in Domesday Book and the area was almost certainly cleared of trees by the eleventh century. Why was it then called the Wolds?

Chris Wickham's idea was that the word *wald* may have come from the Latin *gualdus*, referring not to vegetation but to the rights held over the land during the post-Roman centuries. These areas existed all over Europe and were usually marginal tracts invariably in royal hands but with common rights of access and exploitation. He describes how these rights were eroded in the Weald in Kent as settlements encroached onto the former woodland and pasture in the centuries before the Norman Conquest. The crucial thing about Wickham's theory is that these rights may have originated in the Roman period when these areas were distinctive zones whose land was held directly by the imperial authority. It may be that it was the unique landholding rights held on the Wolds during the Roman centuries that coloured the way that they were exploited and managed right up to the Middle Ages.

THE WOLDS TODAY

You don't have to be an archaeologist or historian to recognise that the Wolds are different. The lack of trees, the regularity of the rectangular fields, the wide roadways and verges, the distant views and dry valleys all combine to open up

73 The managed plantations are often used
for rearing and shooting game birds. Here
is a gun marker and pheasant feeder at
Cow Dale near Huggate

the horizon and force you to take stock of your surroundings (*73, 74* and *75*).
These aspects of the landscape are a combination of the topography and long-
term history of the place. The two cannot be separated.

When I began to think about writing this book, I wanted to find out about
how the people who live here today thought about the Wolds. This book
has been about the landscape but also about how communities perceived
their surroundings and their past. This story is still unfolding, so I sent out
questionnaires to everyone and anyone I could find who lived on the Wolds
today. This was a random survey but an informative one. I received responses
from landowners and farmers but also from villagers and outsiders, commuters
and shop owners. There was a remarkable consistency in the attitude of the
respondents towards the scenery and atmosphere of the Wolds. One person
remarked: 'The aspect is vast, cold and lonesome. One can walk for several miles
and not see a soul.' There was a feeling that tourists and walkers had overlooked
this place but this lack of people is actually what many people enjoyed. 'Most
people tend to think in terms of the North York Moors, the Lake District or the
Peaks, which is why you meet so few people when you're out walking.' However

there were also those who considered there were too many visitors using the place for leisure. The agent of a large country estate commented, 'The place is farmed mostly very well but that does not suit the urbanites who tend to see it as a public park.'

Everybody who responded was aware of the huge changes in the population since the Second World War. Local folk who had been brought up here felt that far fewer people today worked on the land and that villages had become inhabited by outsiders commuting to work in Beverley, York or Hull. Similarly the range of local services in these villages has dropped in living memory. One North Dalton resident remembered: 'When I was a child there was a cobblers, two pubs, two shops, a fish and chip shop, a joiners, a blacksmiths and a church. Now there is only a church and a pub in the village.' For every viewpoint, there was always a contradictory opinion. One villager welcomed the influx of outsiders into villages as he felt they had breathed new life into the communities, introducing new outlooks and interests.

I asked about farming in the questionnaire and everyone replied that this has become massively more mechanised and intensive in the last few decades. The farmers felt that the open spaces were well suited to this kind of farming and said that the land is farmed very well. Other respondents highlighted how much

Opposite: 74 The Wolds is used by many people for recreation. Here, two of the most popular walking routes intersect

Right: 75 Walking on the Wolds can be a solitary experience

had changed since the last century. They lamented that chemical fertilisers and pesticides had replaced the old system where the land was enriched on a small-scale through crop rotation and manure from livestock. Another respondent felt that the use of crop spraying had devastated local wildlife, namely insects, wildflowers and birds.

It was interesting to hear people's views on the history of the landscape. Many felt it had been wooded heavily until the Middle Ages when it was taken in to arable cultivation. Others thought that the Wolds had been cultivated during prehistory only to revert to pasture after the Roman occupation. Without exception, the respondents all felt extremely lucky to live there. 'I love it. I love the way the hills all roll together to form ravines' was how one person put it.

The place has changed since the Second World War and things are changing still. The unending story of this landscape is still being told. This quick snapshot of local people's views shows that even today, when we can get close to people's perceptions, they are not all the same. For one individual, a change will be for the good whereas for someone else, it will be detrimental. This has always been so and any attempt to understand the past with a single outlook is missing this fact. For some people the recent ban on hunting with hounds will adversely affect the Wolds landscape, as it will take away revenue and tradition. For others, it will pave the way for more humane pursuits and help to heal the cultural rift that exists between town and country. These debates are part of the unfolding social history of the people who live here and their outcome will have an effect on the landscape, for these people and their lives are a part of it. The long-term story we have told is the only way to include the modern world and to forge a relationship between the past and the present. This story has not been about battles or coronations but about local communities and their place in the changing landscape. The story of generations of Wolds' people has been told through the places they inhabited and knew.

FURTHER READING

1 ARCHAEOLOGY, LANDSCAPE AND LONG-TERM HISTORY

Allison, K. *The East Riding of Yorkshire Landscape* Hodder and Stoughton, 1976

Hoskins, W. *The Making of the English Landscape* Hodder and Stoughton, 1988

Manby, T., Moorhouse, S. and Ottaway, P. (eds) *The Archaeology of Yorkshire: An assessment at the beginning of the 21st century* Yorkshire Archaeology Society, 2003

Van de Noort, R. *The Humber Wetlands: The Archaeology of a Dynamic Landscape* Wingather Press, 2004

Hayfield, C. and Wagner, P. 'From Dolines to Dewponds: a study of water supplies on the Yorkshire Wolds', *Landscape History* v 17 pp.49-65, 1995

Manby, T. (ed.) *Archaeology in Eastern Yorkshire: Essays in honour of TCM Brewster* University of Sheffield Dept of Archaeology and Prehistory, 1988

Mortimer, J.R. *Forty Years Researches in British and Saxon Burial Mounds of East Yorkshire* Brown and sons, Hull, 1905

Rackham, O. *The History of the Countryside* Duncan Baird, 1994

Stoertz, C. *Ancient Landscapes of the Yorkshire Wolds: aerial photographic transcription and analysis* Royal Commission on the Historical monuments of England, 1997

2 THE EARLIEST BOUNDARIES AT THE BEGINNING OF THE FIRST MILLENNIUM BC

Bowen, C. and Fowler, P. (eds) *Early Land Allotment*. British Archaeological Reports 48, 1978

Barrett, J. *Fragments From Antiquity* Blackwell, 1994

Bradley, R., Entwhistle, R. and Raymond, F. (eds) *Prehistoric Land Divisions on Salisbury Plain: The Work of the Wessex Linear Ditches Project* English Heritage, 1994

Ehrenberg, M. and Caple, C. *Excavations at Fimber, East Yorkshire* Yorkshire Archaeology Society Prehistory Section Bulletin, 1985

Fleming, A. *The Dartmoor Reaves* Batsford, 1988

Grantham, C. and Grantham, E. 'An Earthwork and Anglian Cemetery at Garton-on-the-Wolds, East Yorkshire' *Yorkshire Archaeological Journal* v 41 pp.355-360, 1965

Manby, T. 'Bronze Age settlement in Eastern Yorkshire' in Barrett, J. and Bradley, R. (eds), *The British Later Bronze Age* pp.307-364. British Archaeological Reports, 1980

Maule-Cole, E. *Notes on the Ancient Entrenchments in the neighbourhood of Wetwang* Proceedings of the Yorkshire Geological and Polytechnic Society v 11 pp.45-53, 1888

Powlesland, D. *Staple Howe in its Landscape,* in Manby, T. (ed.), *Archaeology in Eastern Yorkshire* pp.101–108. University of Sheffield, Dept Archaeology, 1988

Spratt, D.A. *Linear Earthworks of the Tabular Hills of Northeast Yorkshire* Department of Archaeology and Prehistory, University of Sheffield, 1989

3 LANDSCAPES OF THE DEAD: CEMETERIES, PASTURES AND TRACKWAYS, *c.*500 BC–AD 70

Bevan, B. *Bounding the Landscape: place and identity during the Yorkshire Wolds Iron Age* in Gwilt, A. and Haselgrove, C. (eds) *Reconstructing Iron Age Societies* Oxbow, 1997

Bevan, B. 'Death in the Landscape: the landscape context of the Iron Age square barrow burials of East Yorkshire' in Downes, J. and Pollard, S. (eds) *The Loved Body's Corruption* Cruithne Press, 1999

Dent, J. *Cemeteries and Settlement Patterns on the Yorkshire Wolds* Proceedings of the Prehistoric Society v 48 pp.437–8, 1982

Dent, J. *A summary of the excavations carried out in Garton Slack and Wetwang Slack* 1964-1980 East Riding Archaeologist v 7 pp.1-14, 1983

Giles, M. *'Open-weave, Close-knit'. Archaeologies of Identity in the Later Prehistoric Landscape of East Yorkshire* Sheffield University: unpublished PhD thesis, 2000

Halkon, P. and Millett, M. *Rural Settlement and Industry: Studies in the Iron Age and Roman Archaeology of Lowland East Yorkshire* Yorkshire Archaeological Report No. 4, 1999

Stead, I. *The Arras Culture* Yorkshire Philosophical Society, 1979

—— *Iron Age Cemeteries in East Yorkshire* English Heritage, 1991

4 FROM ROUNDHOUSES TO VILLAS: ROMANISED AGRICULTURAL LANDSCAPES, FIRST–FIFTH CENTURIES AD

Bishop, T. 'An Iron Age and Romano-British ladder settlement at Melton, East Yorkshire' *Yorkshire Archaeological Journal* v 71 pp.23-63, 1999

Hayfield, C. *An Archaeological Survey of the Parish of Wharram Percy, East Yorkshire: 1 The evolution of the Roman landscape* British Archaeological Reports, 1987

Hunter-Mann, K. *Excavations on a Roman extra-mural settlement at Brough on Humber, East Yorkshire UK* Internet Archaeology http://intarch.ac.uk/journal/issue9/brough_index.html 2000

Price, J., Wilson, D. and Evans, D. (eds) *Recent Research in Roman Yorkshire* British Archaeological Reports, 1988

Ramm, H. *The Parisi* Duckworth, 1978

Stead, I.M. *Rudston Roman Villa* Yorkshire Archaeology Society, 1980

5 SETTLEMENT PATTERNS AND RURAL ESTATES ON THE POST–ROMAN WOLDS

Eagles, B. *The Anglo-Saxon Settlement of Humberside* British Archaeological Reports 68, 1979

Faull, M. 'Late Anglo-Saxon Settlement Patterns in Yorkshire' in Faull, M. (ed.) *Studies in late Anglo-Saxon settlement* Oxford, 1984

Faull, M. and Stinson, M. (eds) *Domesday Book: Yorkshire* Phillimore, 1986

Jones, G. 'Multiple Estates and Early Settlement' in Sawyer, P. (ed.) *Medieval Settlement: Continuity and Change* Arnold, 1976

Powlesland, D. *Excavations at Heslerton: The Anglian Cemetery* Landscape Research Centre, 2002

Powlesland, D., Haughton, C. and Hanson, J. 'Excavations at Heslerton, North Yorkshire 1978-1982' *Archaeological Journal* v 143 pp.53-173, 1986

Rahtz, P. 'Anglo-Saxon Yorkshire: current research problems' in Geake, H. and Kenny, J. (eds) *Early Deira: Archaeological Studies of the East Riding in the Fourth to the Ninth Centuries AD* Oxbow Books pp.1-10, 2000

Richards, J. *Cottam: An Anglian and Anglo-Scandinavian settlement on the Yorkshire Wolds* Yorkshire Archaeological Journal v 156 pp.1-110, 1999

Smith, A.H. *The Place-names of the East Riding of Yorkshire and York* English Place-Name Society, 1937

Watkin, T. *The Archaeology of Anglian East Yorkshire* East Riding Archaeologist v 7, 1983

FURTHER READING

6 IN SEARCH OF THE PASTORAL WOLDS

Farrer, W. *Early Yorkshire Charters* Privately printed, 1914

Fox, H. 'The people of the Wolds in English Settlement History' in Aston, M., Austin, D. and Dyer, C. (eds), *The Rural Settlements of Medieval England* Blackwell, 1989

Fox, H. 'The Wolds before 1500' in Thirsk, J. (ed.) *Rural England: an illustrated history of the landscape* Oxford University Press, 2000

Le Patourel, H., Long, M. and Pickles, M. (eds) *Yorkshire Boundaries* Yorkshire Archaeology Society, 1993

Loveluck, C.P. 'The Development of the Anglo-Saxon Landscape, Economy and Society 'On Driffield', East Yorkshire, 400-750 AD *Anglo-Saxon Studies in Archaeology and History* vol 9 pp.25-48, 1999

Lucy, S. *The Early Anglo-Saxon Cemeteries of East Yorkshire: An analysis and reinterpretation* British Archaeological Reports, 1998

Reynolds, A. 'On execution sites and cemeteries' in de Boe, G. and Verhaege, F. (eds) *Death and Burial in Medieval Europe* pp.34-41 IAP, 1997

Semple, S. 'A fear of the past: the place of the prehistoric burial mound in the ideology of middle and later Anglo-Saxon England' *World Archaeology* v 30 pp.109-126, 1998

Wickham, C. 'European Forests in the early Middle Ages' *Settimane di Studio* v 37 pp.479-548 1989

7 ANOTHER TURN OF THE CYCLE: THE MEDIEVAL LANDSCAPE AND THE AGE OF ENCLOSURE

Beresford, M. and Hurst, J. *Wharram Percy: Deserted Medieval Village* Batsford/English Heritage, 1990

Brooks, F.W. *Domesday Book and the East Riding* East Yorkshire Local History Society, 1986

Crowther, J. (ed.) *Descriptions of Est Yorkshire: de la Pryme to Head* East Yorkshire Local History Society, 1992

English, B. *Great Landowners of East Yorkshire* Harvester Wheatsheaf, 1991

Harris, A. *The Rural Landscape of the East Riding of Yorkshire:* 1700-1850 Oxford University Press, 1969

Harvey, M. 'Regular open-field systems on the Yorkshire Wolds', *Landscape History* v 4 pp.29-39, 1982

Sheppard, J. 'Medieval Village Planning in northern England: some evidence from Yorkshire', *Journal of Historical Geography* v 2 pp.3-20, 1976

Williamson, T. *Shaping Medieval Landscapes* Windgather Press, 2002

Woodward, D. (ed.) *Descriptions of East Yorkshire: Leland to Defoe* East Yorkshire Local History Society, 1985

8 RHYTHMIC CYCLES OF LIFE AND LANDSCAPE

Bradley, R. 'Time Regained: The Creation of Continuity', *Journal of the British Archaeological Association* v 140 pp.1-17, 1987

Bradley, R. *The Past in Prehistoric Societies* Routledge, 2002

Fenton-Thomas, C. *Late Prehistoric and Early Historic Landscapes on the Yorkshire Chalk* British Archaeological Reports 350 Archaeopress, 2003

INDEX

If you are interested in purchasing other books published by Tempus,
or in case you have difficulty finding any Tempus books in your local bookshop,
you can also place orders directly through our website

www.tempus-publishing.com